A COURSE IN FOOTBALL FOR PLAYERS AND COACHES

OFFENSE

A reprint of the 1908 - 1910 pamphlets

Introduction by Tom Benjey

GLENN S. WARNER, ATHLETIC DIRECTOR
INDIAN SCHOOL, CARLISLE, PENNA.

Carlisle, Pennsylvania

All new material copyright 2007 Tuxedo Press

Published by Tuxedo Press
Carlisle, PA 17015
LoneStarDietz.com

All rights reserved. No part of this publication may be reproduced, stored in a retrieval system, or transmitted, in any form or by any means, electronic, mechanical, photocopying, recording, or otherwise, without the prior permission of Tuxedo Press.

ISBN-10 0-9774486-5-7
ISBN-13 978-0-9774486-5-4
Library of Congress Control Number: 2007902238

Table of Contents

		Page
Part I	Introduction	5
Part II	1908 Offense pamphlet	13
	Regular formation	16
	End-back formation	22
	Punt formation	28
Part III	1909 Supplement	37
Part IV	1910 Offense pamphlet	45
	Regular formation	48
	Direct pass formation	56
	Open formation	64
	Punt formation	69

4

Introduction

While researching the life of Lone Star Dietz I read in a September 1906 issue of the Carlisle Indian School newspaper, *The Arrow*, that Pop Warner, then head coach at Cornell, spent a week with the Carlisle coaches, former stars Bemus Pierce and Frank Hudson, preparing them for the upcoming season. I didn't think much about it at the time but remembered it because it seemed a bit odd that Warner would be assisting a potential adversary. Later I read some pieces written by Warner in which he stated that the single-wing had been first used in 1906 and that it was first used at Carlisle but he couldn't remember against which opponent he unleashed it.

Mentioned in various issues of that year's *Arrow* were the major rule changes implemented for the 1906 season in response to President Theodore Roosevelt's threat to ban football after a large number of fatalities and much larger number of serious injuries to players in 1905. Carlisle scheduled a Wednesday contest to precede the usual season start to illustrate a game played under the new rules to coaches and players in the East. A large crowd turned out to see what was billed as "the first important game to be played under the new rules." Modern American football began at 3:00 p.m. Wednesday, September 26, 1906 at Indian Field on Carlisle Barracks when the Indians hosted Villanova. It was very likely that an early form of the single-wing was used by Carlisle in this historic game. Videographer Tom McCue and I made a short documentary to commemorate the 100th anniversary of this game. After publicizing the documentary I was made aware that sportswriter Alison Danzig had dated the single-wing's origin to a later date. His opinion was based largely on a 1931 article in which Warner contradicted himself and a conversation Danzig had with Warner in the 1950s. The College Football Hall of Fame found my documentary interesting but was apparently unaware of the game or Warner's repeated claim that he started using the single-wing or variations of it in 1906.

Direct Snap, a website for single-wing devotees, independently arrived at 1906 as the 100th anniversary of Warner's offense likely based on his writings and some newspaper articles that described a formation Cornell ran that year. It made sense to me that Warner would run an offense at Cornell similar to the one he taught to the Indians. After all, how many new offenses could he have invented in the months that had passed since the drastic rule changes were made? In Warner's case that could be a lot, but we'll put that issue aside for now.

Ted Seay and Todd Bross made me aware of Danzig's claim and suggested I look at contemporaneous literature to nail down the date of the single-wing's birth. Newspaper articles were inconclusive. Reporters wrote a lot about the open play of the Indians under the new rules but didn't really say anything about the formations they used. One pundit thought football played under the new rules more closely resembled basketball. Another thought it effeminate. The most contemporaneous thing I had from Warner was his 1912 book that showed a balanced-line single-wing and other direct-snap formations. Ted and Todd recommended that I find a copy of Warner's 1908 correspondence course, *A Course in Football for Players and Coaches* to see what offensive formations he was teaching. Finding a copy proved easier said than done. Of course the Library of Congress has it but they won't let it out on interlibrary loan, but for a nonrefundable charge of $14 and an 8 to 10 week delay (longer if they're busy) they will estimate what the photocopying charges would be. I eventually stumbled across a copy in the Notre Dame library.

George Rugg sent me photocopies of the Offense pamphlet and in it I found diagrams for plays from multiple offensive sets. The first set of plays were from what Warner called the "regular formation," an old-style T-formation with the quarterback behind, not under, center but a yard or so behind him. The fullback was a little deeper than the halfbacks. The quarterback received the snap from center and distributed the ball to other backs, threw a forward pass or ran around the end. In 1908 the back who received the snap from center was not allowed to carry the ball up the middle.

Next I came across what Warner called his "end-back formation." Because the 1906 rules only required six men on the line of scrimmage, Warner put his left end behind the gap between right guard and tackle as a blocking back, sort of. He left the quarterback behind center. Warner put the right halfback on a wing outside right end. The fullback was shifted over to the right halfback's position in the "regular formation" and the left halfback took the position formerly occupied by the fullback. See figure No. 7 in the 1908 Offense pamphlet for an illustration of this formation.

The "end-back formation" is the earliest documented use of a wingback by Glenn Warner. That is not to say that he or someone else didn't used wingbacks earlier. Other formations are also included in this pamphlet. Warner diagrammed a series of plays from punt formation, including direct snaps to up-backs and snaps that lead the deep back. The pamphlet that was copied appeared to be incomplete as I received plays 1 through 18, 20 and 31 through 35. I assumed that some pages were missing and ordered a copy of the pamphlet from Springfield College. When it arrived I was surprised to see that it had no copyright date and was not the same pamphlet as it had a different opening narrative and different plays.

I then located another copy of Warner's correspondence course. This one was in the Exendine papers at the University of Tulsa. Albert Exendine had been a star end at Carlisle when Warner was developing his new offense and had gone on to become a successful coach in his own right. The Exendine files contained two offense pamphlets: one with the 1908 copyright date and one with no date. The Offense pamphlet with no copyright date on it was significantly different from the 1908 version and was complete. The 1908 version was the same as the one from Notre Dame except it did not have the five pages covering plays 31 through 35. When I looked at them I noticed that plays 31 through 35 had page numbers 2 through 5 on them. A light came on. The extra pages were likely a 1909 supplement. George Rugg graciously looked through the Notre Dame files and found that the other side of Play 31, page 2, was titled, "Offense: Supplement" and had page number 1. After looking at the file closely, he concluded that this pamphlet probably never had a cover. This implied that the extra five plays were a supplement that was published after 1908, but in what year?

The five plays in the supplement were variations on five of the plays in the 1908 Offense pamphlet that were executed from the "end-back formation." Each of the five started off like one of the earlier plays but developed differently. The "Old Fox" was inserting more deception into his scheme. At least one of these plays, No. 35, had been used successfully by the Carlisle Indians. We know that because Warner wrote, "This play is being used successfully by the Indians…"

George Rugg found Play No. 19 in the Defense pamphlet, probably because it deals mostly with defending punts including fake punts. Warner probably had his own reasons for numbering this 19. It is not included herein because the same play can be found on page 140 of Warner's 1912 book.

I then turned my attention to the pamphlets from Springfield College and the University of Tulsa which had no copyright dates and found them to be the same. In the second paragraph of the pamphlet, Pop opined that the then current rule changes would eliminate the direct pass from the center to the quarterback for most teams. He also mentioned that pushing and pulling the ball carrier was no longer allowed. Most likely he was referring to the 1910 rule changes. So, this pamphlet was surely intended for coaches preparing for the 1910 season. Because the supplement included earlier formations, it was probably from 1909.

As had the 1908 Offense pamphlet, the undated one contained a series of plays from the "regular formation" but this time the fullback was forward of the halfbacks, almost like in a wishbone. In figure No. 8 was a "direct pass formation in which the backs are massed upon one side of the ball." The formation wasn't named but it was a balanced-line single-wingback formation. The left halfback (tailback) stood four and a half to five yards behind the line aligned with the gap between center and left guard. Back 3 (fullback) stood a little closer to the line behind the right guard. Back 2 (blocking back) stood two and a half yards behind the line and in the gap between right guard and tackle. Back 4 (wingback) stood outside his right end and behind the line.

Warner described play No. 10, a short end run, as "a very effective ground gainer." This statement implies that he had tested this play in an important game prior to 1910. Although the tailback received a direct snap from center, he likely headed upfield five yards down the line from where the ball was snapped. Thus, this play would have been legal years prior as would many of the single-wing plays in this pamphlet. It was just the player receiving the snap who could not carry the ball up the middle. He would have had to hand off to someone else to do that. As we well know, the single-wing had more than its share of fakes and handoffs.

So, Pop Warner definitely had released the direct snap single-wing to the world before 1912, in 1910 most likely, and had probably run it himself well before that. Many of the plays he diagrammed in the 1910 version of the correspondence course would have been legal in 1906, so he might well have started using them immediately after the major rules change. Also, it is unlikely that he risked his reputation by including untried plays in his correspondence course. And the "Old Fox" probably didn't share his latest tricks until his competitors had become familiar with them. It seems to me that Warner did indeed start using a version of the single-wing in 1906 and tinkered with it for years to come. As a footnote, a *Philadelphia Press* reporter interviewed Warner after the 1910 Carlisle-Penn game and asked Warner about his use of direct snaps. Warner responded that he used direct snap formations exclusively that year. This means he did not use the "regular formation" that he spent so much time on in his correspondence course and it doesn't mean that he didn't use direct snap formations in prior years. It also doesn't mean that he hadn't used direct snap formations exclusively in earlier years. Those questions were not asked.

One of my information sources was a letter from Warner to Col. A. M. Weyand, football historian and Captain of the 1915 West Point team, written in the early 1950s in which Warner told Weyand that he started using the single-wing in 1906. I recently came across a copy of A. M. Weyand's 1955 book, *The Saga of American Football* and found something relevant in it. On page 99, Weyand wrote, "There was one coach who was never at a loss as to what procedure to follow. That was Pop Warner. In 1907 he had begun using a wing back and a direct pass from center. He brought the single-wing system into general use when the rules authorized the first receiver of the ball from center to cross the line of scrimmage at any point. At first he called it his 'backs over, direct pass formation.' Other coaches used systems of a somewhat similar nature, but Warner was the first to popularize this style of play."

In the Foreword to Weyand's book, Grantland Rice wrote, "He takes the same pains to be accurate and thorough that research scholars take in other fields. Consequently, he is probably the foremost living authority on football." These would seem to be very strong credentials.

My opinion as to why Weyand placed the birth of the single-wing at 1907 is that he didn't know about Warner's 1906 visit to Carlisle. He was likely well aware that Warner returned to Carlisle in 1907 as athletic director and attributed Warner's 1906 assertion to poor memory.

After finishing this introduction and laying out this book, Michael Salmon, Librarian for the Amateur Athletic Foundation of Los Angeles, found a copy of Warner's correspondence course in their collection. It includes a copy of the 1908 Offense pamphlet and the 1909 Supplement. The supplement contains one more page, play 35, than the Notre Dame copy and includes its cover. While preparing this book for publication I visited the Library of Congress and looked at their copy of the correspondence course. They have bound the 1908 version of the pamphlets as a hardback book. So, all known versions of the offense pamphlet have been viewed and are included in this book. That is not to say that something else exists that may surface in the future. If something does, this book will be revised to include it.

Copies of Warner's correspondence course are rarely found. Because the pamphlets were initially published as a correspondence course, they were not purchased by libraries and placed in their collections. Those copies that have been located found their way into archives as parts of collections donated to or purchased by the libraries. Most were likely discarded by coaches when they were considered outdated.

This book is the first of a trilogy of reprints of Pop Warner's documentation of the development of the single-wing offense. The second is his 1912 compilation of his latest version of the correspondence course into book form. Confusingly, this book is also titled, *A Course in Football for Players and Coaches*. In 1927 he updated his book to include unbalanced line single-wing and double-wing formations. By that time these formations had been used long enough that he wasn't giving away his secrets. That book was titled, not surprisingly, *Football for Coaches and Players*. It was also illustrated by Warner's protégé, Lone Star Dietz. That book ends with the words:

> *Don't ever think that you can't win it,*
> *A fightin' team is always in it.*
> *So don't let up a single minute,*
>   *Keep a-goin'!*

Tom Benjey
May 2007

A COURSE IN FOOTBALL
FOR PLAYERS AND COACHES

OFFENSE

Copyright 1908 by G. S. Warner

GLENN S. WARNER, ATHLETIC DIRECTOR
INDIAN SCHOOL, CARLISLE, PENNA.

This shows correct positions of the players upon regular formation ready for the ball to be snapped, except that the quarter should have his hands extended toward the ball, instead of upon his knees.

Offense

EVERY team's offense should consist of a limited number of first class plays, perfectly mastered, and of sufficient variety to enable it to meet any style of defense under all sorts of conditions, and be able to take advantage of any weakness which might develop in the defense of opposing teams. No team should depend upon one style of attack. The offensive strength should consist of straight, powerful line plays, end runs with perfectly formed interference, two or three fake plays which have some power in them, and do not depend entirely upon deceiving the opponents, two or three good forward pass plays, and several plays from the punt formation. These should be combined with ability to kick field goals, and an onside kick or two might be of value, although the forward pass can easily be made to serve for the latter.

Many teams are unwisely taught a large number of plays—so many that it is impossible to master them all thoroughly, and often resulting in confusion of signals. It is much better to have a few good plays well learned, than to have a large assortment imperfectly worked up and some of which are likely to be of doubtful strength. The more important and harder the game the fewer plays are used, because the team has the ball less, has to punt more, and when rushing the ball only uses a select few of its strongest plays.

Trick plays are useful to add variety to the attack, to keep the opponents guessing and thus aid the regular plays, and occasionally to pull off a long run, but they should not be depended upon to win games, and only a few good ones should be taught the players.

In diagraming the following plays, care has been taken to select only those which have been proven in important games to be good ones. Many more might be explained, but the list here diagramed is large enough, and varied enough, to enable any team to select from it a powerful, scientific and varied attack, which will succeed against the defense of any team in its class.

The plays are diagramed upon five yard squares, so that the approximate distances can be seen at a glance, and each play is only diagramed for one side of the line. How the same play should be played on the opposite side, can easily be figured out by studying the diagrams, or by copying the plays upon a thin sheet of paper, holding to the light, and looking at the reverse side. The man who carries the ball is indicated by the solid black circle. The defensive back, who plays in the extreme back-field to handle punts, etc., is not shown in the diagrams.

There are six plays diagramed for one side of the line from the regular formation, or twelve in all; six diagrams, or twelve plays from the end-back formation; and five diagrams, or ten plays from the punt formation. This furnishes a total of thirty-four selected plays, without counting the punt, drop-kick, or quick place-kick. Twenty good plays are enough for any team, and no team should have over twenty-five.

The regular simple formation plays and the punts should be given the team as early as possible, and the forward passes and other plays should then be mastered at the rate of about two or three each week.

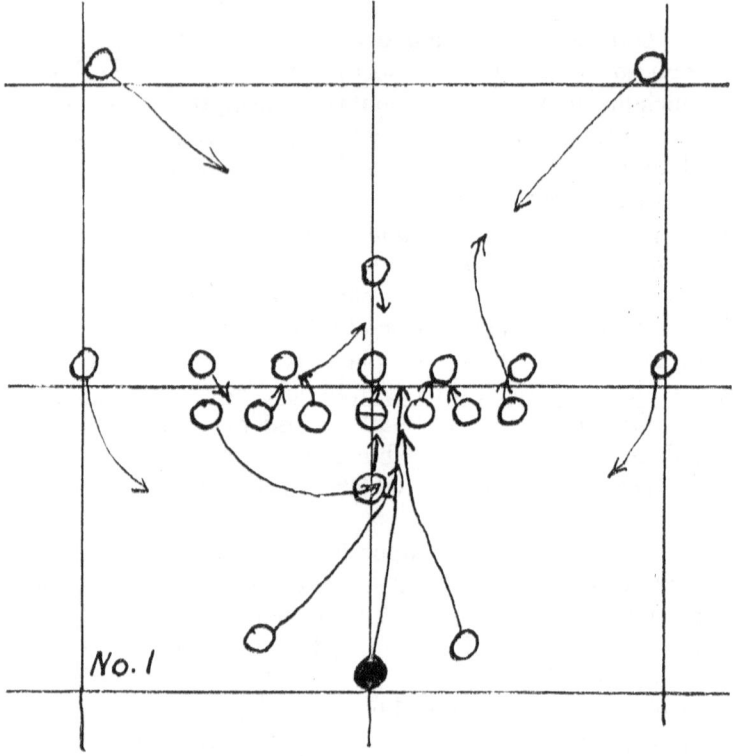

No. 1. In this play full-back carries the ball between the opposing center and left guard. Left half should be pushing with his shoulder upon the full-back's right hip, and right half upon the other. Left end should leave his position and push directly from behind. Quarter, after passing the ball, goes into the line at the full-back's side, and helps bend the line backward. Right guard and tackle carry the opposing guard back and to the right. Center charges his man back and to the left. Right end blocks opposing tackle, and goes through and blocks opposing left half, Left tackle and guard force opposing guard away from the play, and then left guard goes through aud blocks a back, or helps the runner.

1908 Offense

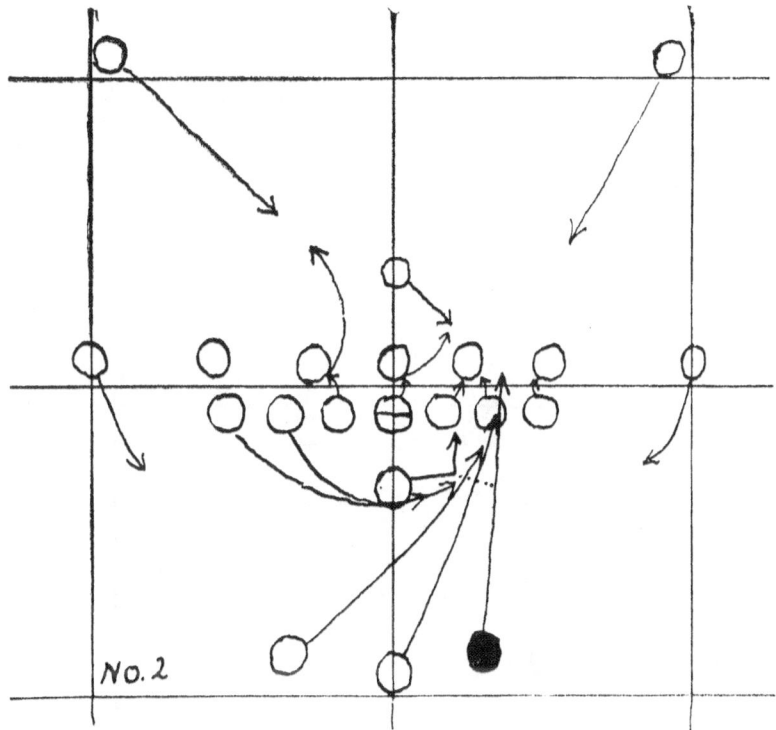

No. 2.—This is one of the strongest plays that can be devised for a sure gain of a few yards. The three backs form a perfect tandem as the man with the ball hits the line, and left tackle and end come behind, making a five-man tandem. In this play the right half should run fairly high and keep his feet, depending more upon the push behind him than upon his own momentum. It is important that the tandem be kept straight. A crooked tandem drives through a good line like a bent pin through a board.

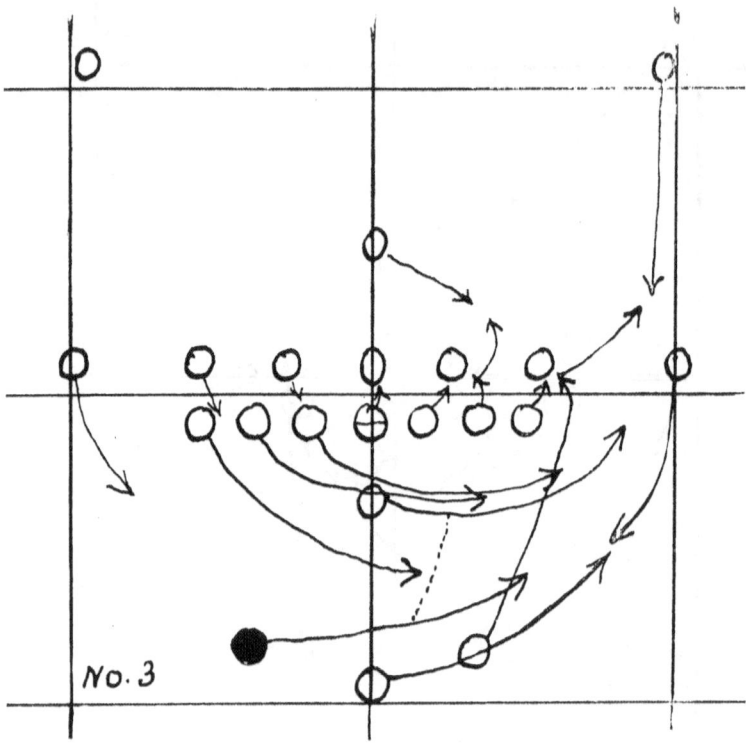

No. 3.—This play is a powerful one, and if well executed, is nearly always sure to gain, and many long runs can be pulled off with it. The play is aimed to go between the opposing tackle and end. The left half should start his run parallel to the line for about three steps, so as to make the opposing end think he intends to go outside. This will allow the full-back to block the end out, just as the runner turns sharply inside of the end and behind his interference, consisting of quarter, left guard, and tackle. Left end follows the play and makes it safe. Right half blocks tackle, but if his end has him safe, he blocks opposing half. Left guard and tackle must leave their positions with the snap of the ball and come around fast. The guard is an important interferer in this play.

1908 Offense 19

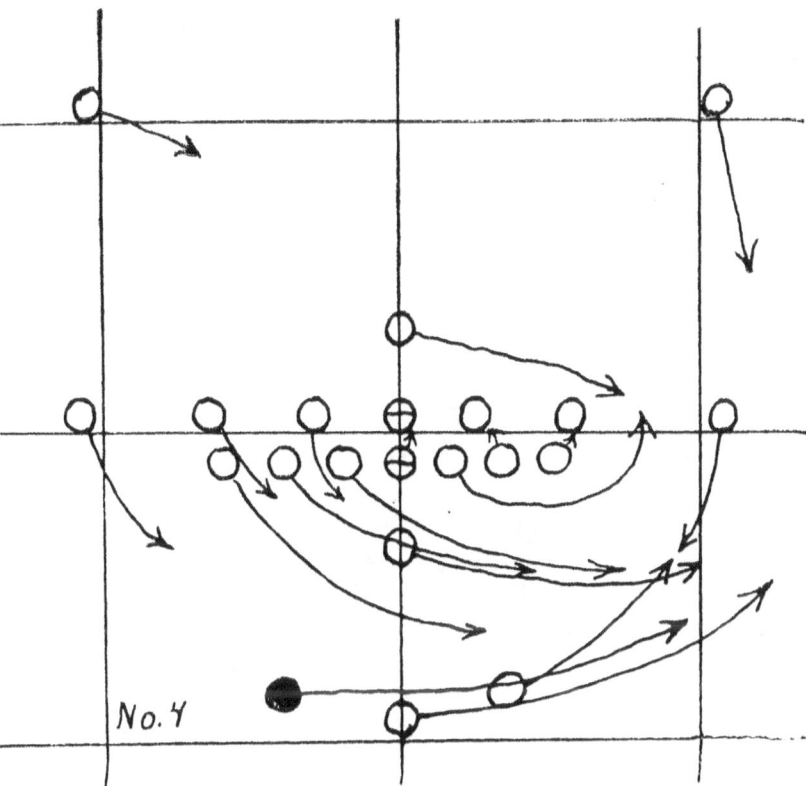

No. 4.—This play is similar to No. 3, but aims to go around the end. Right half blocks the end in, and the interference swings wide. Right guard jumps back and swings around close to line, blocking off the first loose man he meets—usually the tackle or back indicated in the diagram. No. 3 is a better play, but this is a good one, and it is needed to work occasionally as a mixer with No. 3, to keep the end guessing.

1908 Offense

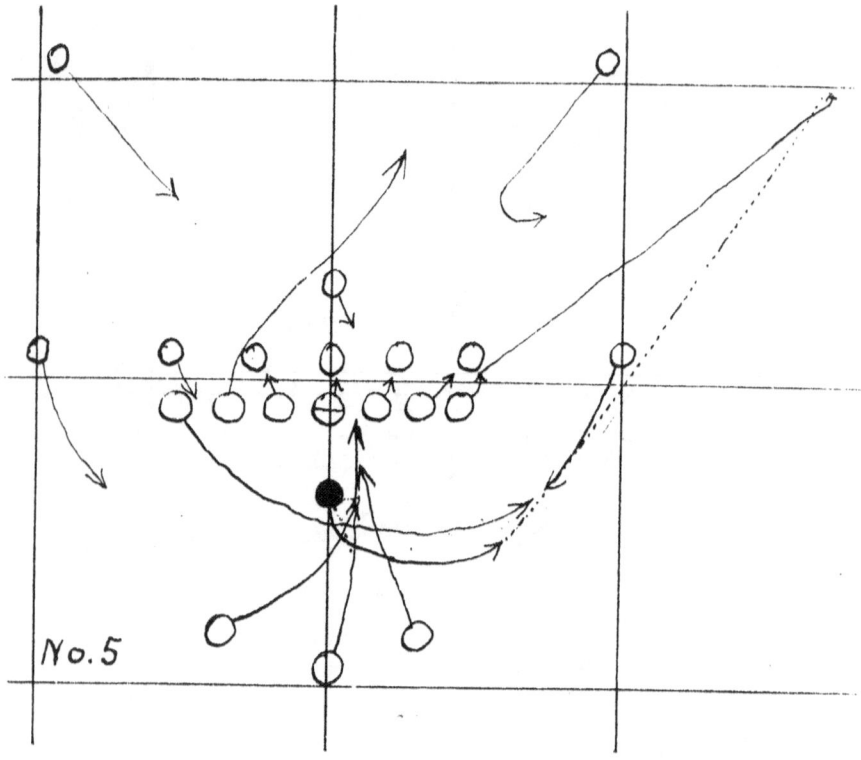

No. 5.—This is a very deceiving play based upon a fake of No. 1, and is as good a trick play as can be devised. Quarter quickly passes ball to full-back and stands with his back to the line, receiving the ball again as the full-back passes. Left half should be directly behind full-back, so as to conceal and not run into the quarter-back. Left end comse around as though to push, but continues around and blocks the opposing left end, quarter following and being careful to start a step or two toward his own goal before turning. Usually the opposing end will be drawn in or blocked, and the quarter can continue for a good gain before passing to the end, who has run out to receive the pass. If about to be tackled by the end, he can pass to his own end as indicated in the diagram. This is a good play without the forward pass at the end of it.

1908 Offense

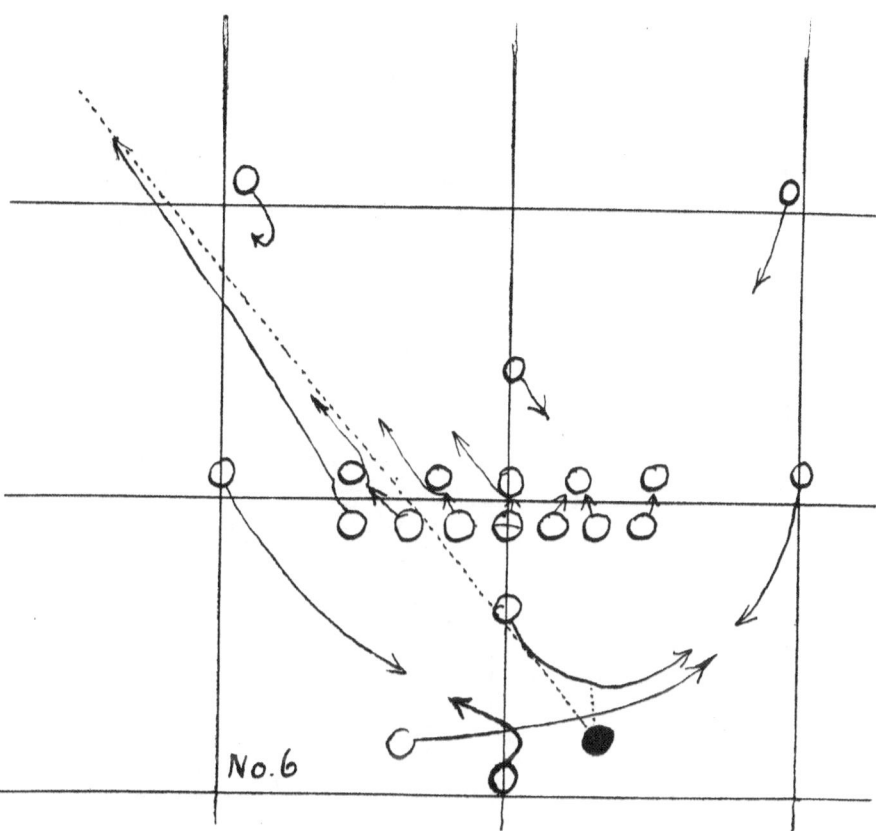

No. 6.—This is a good onside kick. Left half runs fast and holds out his hands as though to receive the ball, then blocks end. Quarter swings back from the line and hands the ball to right half, who has moved back a trifle and laid low. Right half then makes a short low punt to the left, to his left end. Full-back starts one step, and then turns and blocks opposing right end. The line men block, and then run toward the place where the punt is to fall.

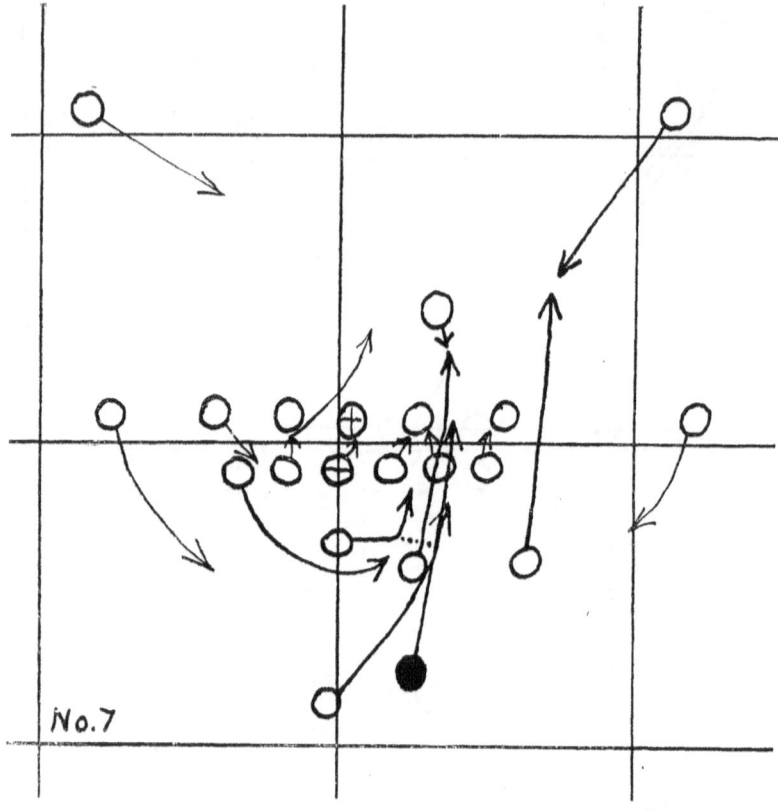

No. 7.—This and following plays are from the end-back formation. An end is drawn back of the line, and one man must be outside of the end of the line. The diagram gives the correct formation. In this play, full-back carries the ball straight ahead. (We will call the man in front of him the left end, and the man outside of the end the right half, in describing these plays, although the men can be arranged differently to suit their qualifications). Left end goes ahead, forces through the line, and blocks off the opposing back. Full-back follows behind him, left half and tackle forming a tandem, pushing from behind. Quarter passes the ball and goes into the line, to help bend it back and to allow left tackle to come around and push. The other men block as indicated in the diagram.

1908 Offense

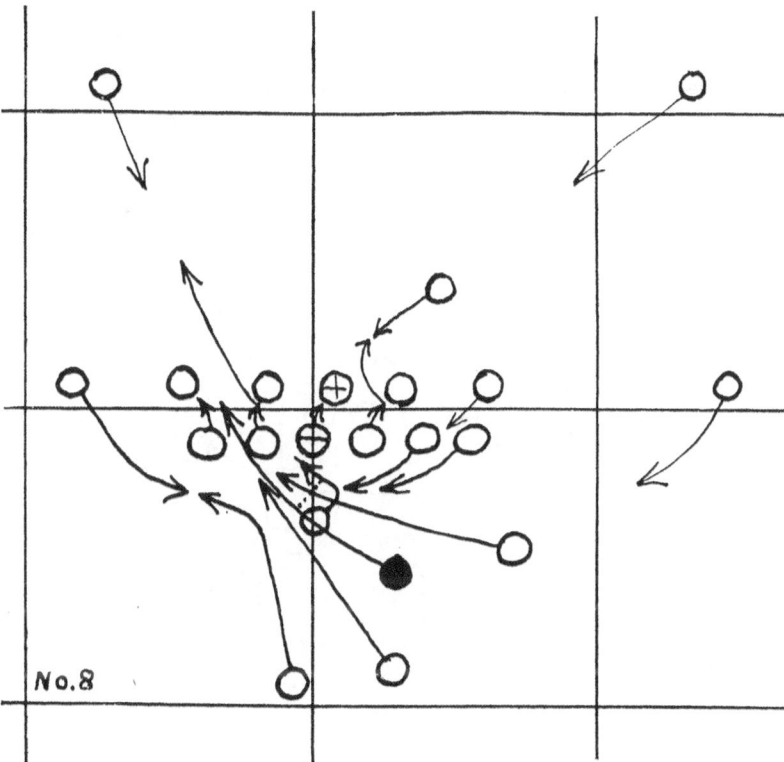

No. 8.—This is a strong cross-buck, left end carrying the ball between opposing right guard and tackle. Full-back, right half, right tackle and end push from behind. Left half blocks opposing end if he is playing in close, otherwise he pushes the runner in. Right guard blocks his man, and goes through and cuts off a back if possible. Quarter goes into the line, so as to allow right tackle and end to get into the play and push.

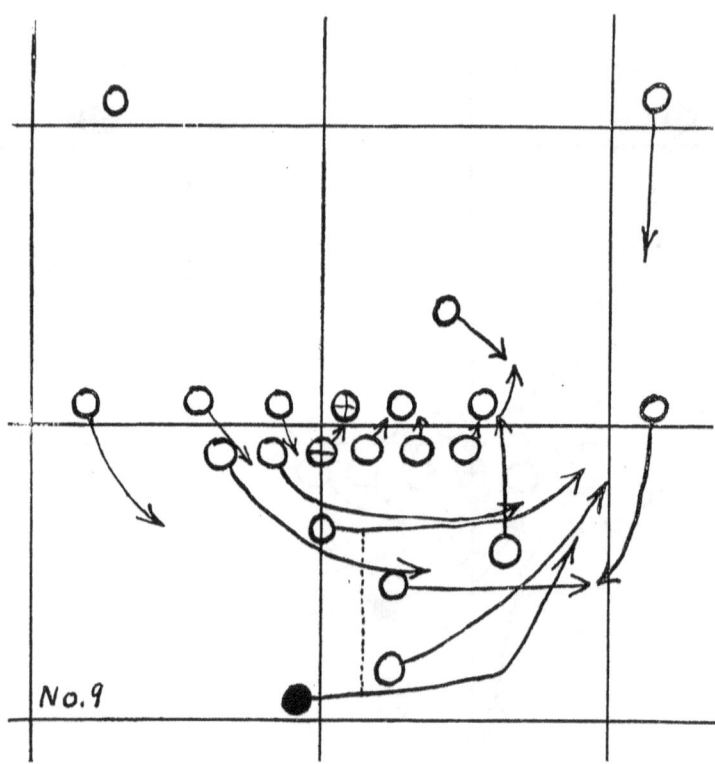

No. 9.—This is about the best ground gaining play that is possible with this formation. It is good for steady gains, and often for long runs. Left end blocks opposing end out. Right half takes tackle if he gets loose, otherwise blocks a back. Left guard, tackle, quarter, and full-back form interference for runner, who takes three steps to the right, parallel to the line to draw the end out, then turns sharply in, as left end blocks the end out. The interference should swing wide enough to allow for their right end being forced back, in case this should happen. If the interferers round the tackle too closely they are liable to be cut off by that player or by their own end being forced back. Right tackle blocks opposing guard or tackle, according to the way they play.

1908 Offense

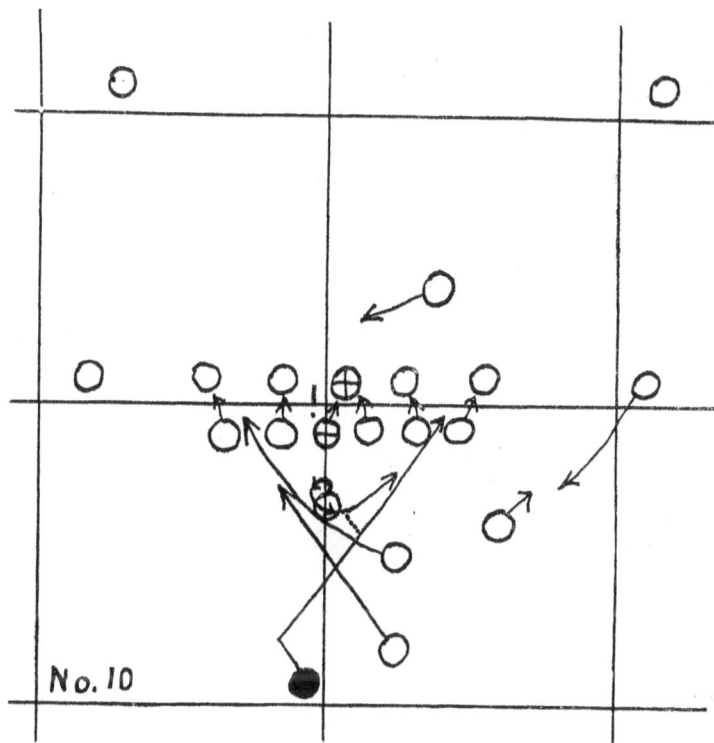

No. 10.—This is a very effective and deceiving fake cross-buck, or split-play. Left end fakes to take the ball as in No. 8, full-back pushing him. Quarter turns to the left and fakes to pass the ball to left end, but continues turning to the left and, with his back to the line, passes the ball to the left half, who has taken one step to the left with his left foot as though to push in the play, all the while keeping close to the ground, and then shooting to the right as indicated, with the quarter pushing him. Right half holds his ground, and blocks the opposing end at the proper moment.

1908 Offense

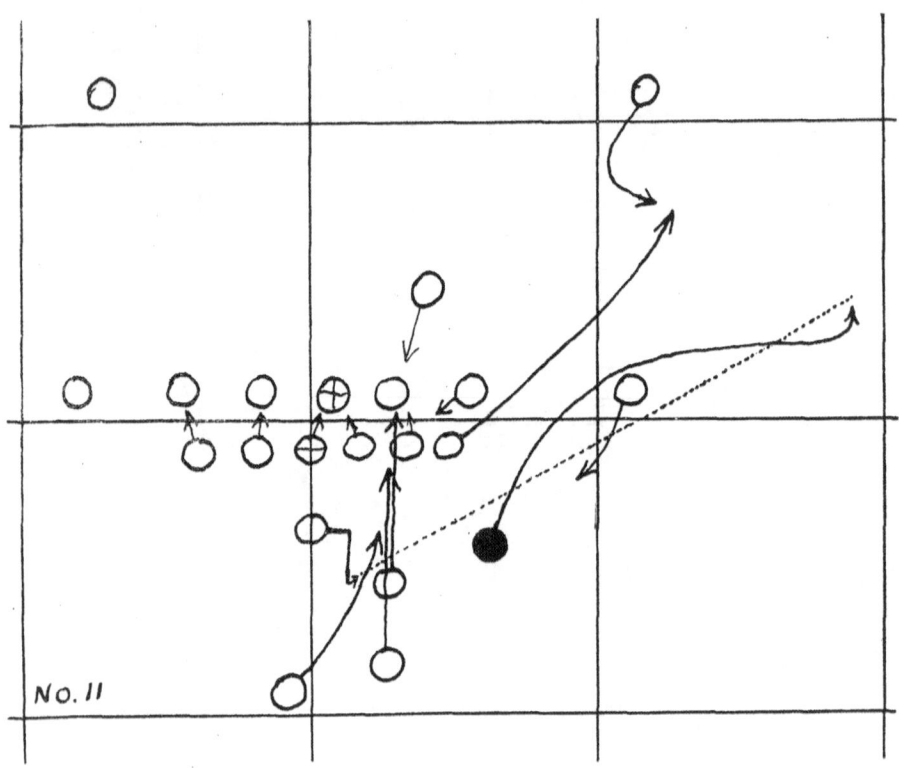

No. 11.—This is a very effective forward pass play. It is made to look exactly like the full-back straight-buck explained by diagram No. 7. The left end, full-back, and left half form a perfect tandem, quarter-back pretending to pass the ball to the full-back who makes a big bluff to take it. Quarter then steps back, and throws the ball out to the right half, who has started forward and then runs out to the side to receive it. Right end goes out to block the opposing back. The quarter should step back far enough, and throw the ball sufficiently to the side, so that it will be sure to cross the line of scrimmage more than five yards from center.

1908 Offense

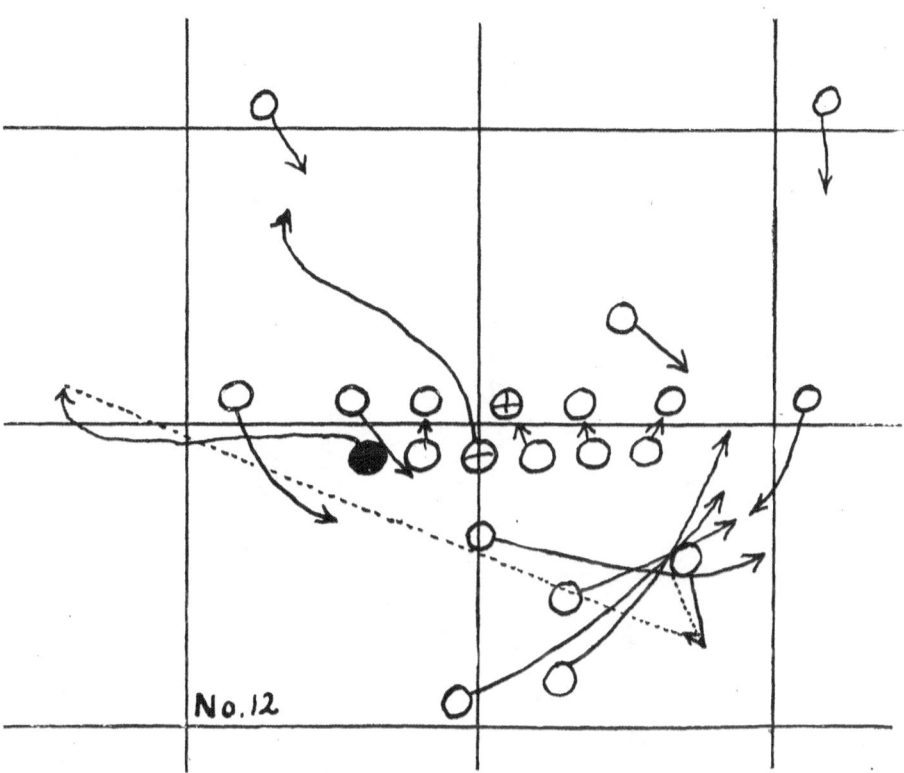

No. 12.—This is a forward pass to the short side. Left end blocks the end, full-back and left half block any opponent coming through outside of tackle. Quarter swings wide, hands the ball to right half and continues on to block the end. Right half backs up, keeps close to the ground, and when handed the ball, passes it wide to the left tackle who has moved out to receive it. The tackle must not be so far forward that the pass will cross the scrimmage line within five yards of center.

28 1908 Offense

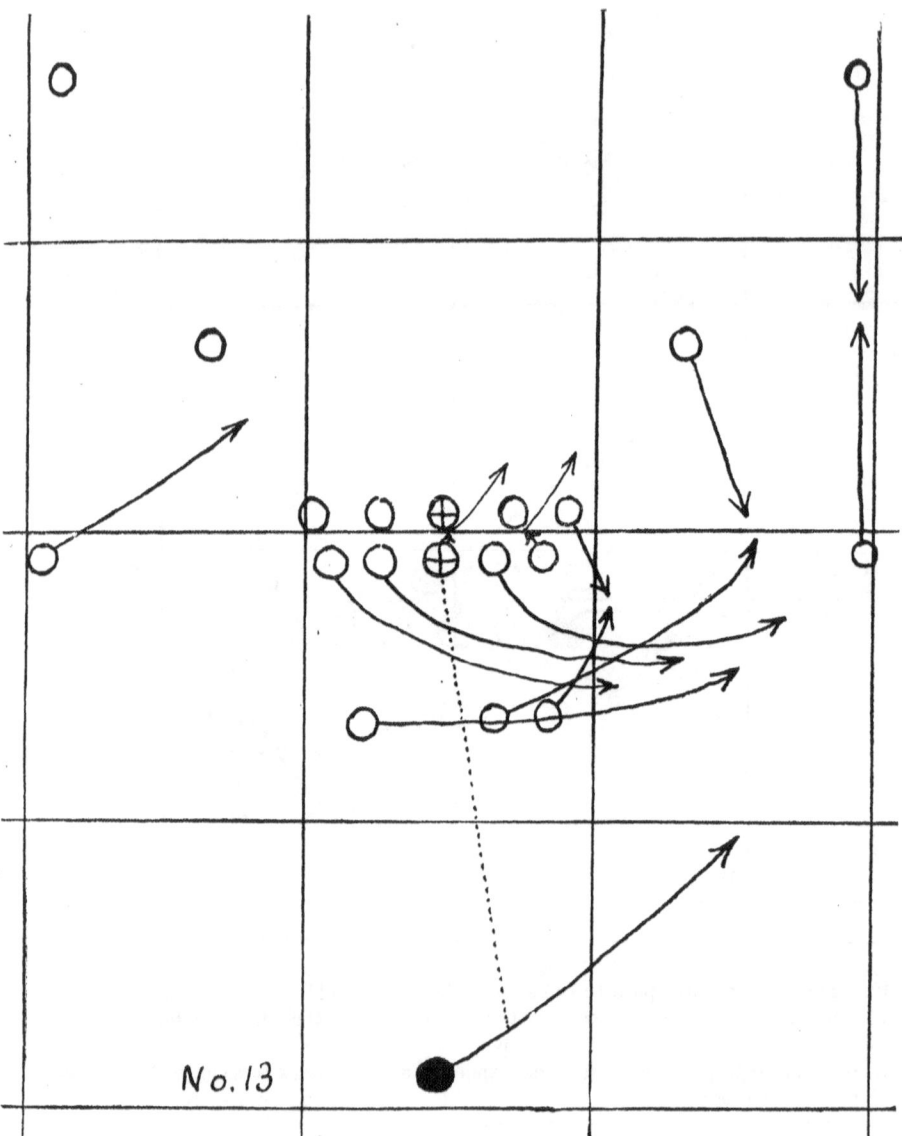

No. 13.—This and following plays are from the punt formation. The center passes the ball to the right, the punter receiving it upon the run. The line men and backs block or interfere as indicated. Speed is a great factor in this play. Note that the right guard gets into the interference, and that right half blocks the opposing tackle. This play starts off like the long forward pass play, or diagram No. 17, and the two are used to help each other and keep the opponent guessing.

1908 Offense

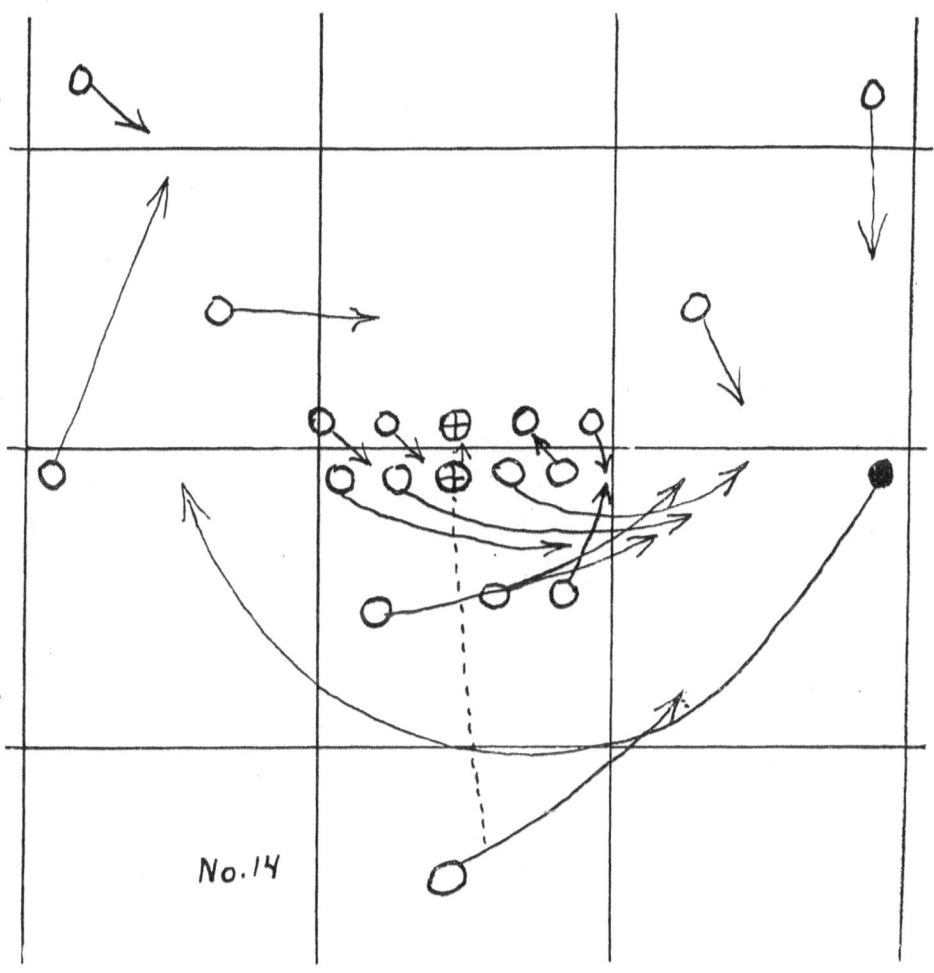

No. 14.—This play starts off like No. 13, but the man receiving the ball passes it to right end, who leaves his position with the snap of the ball and swings around the opposite end. This is a criss-cross that works.

30   1908 Offense

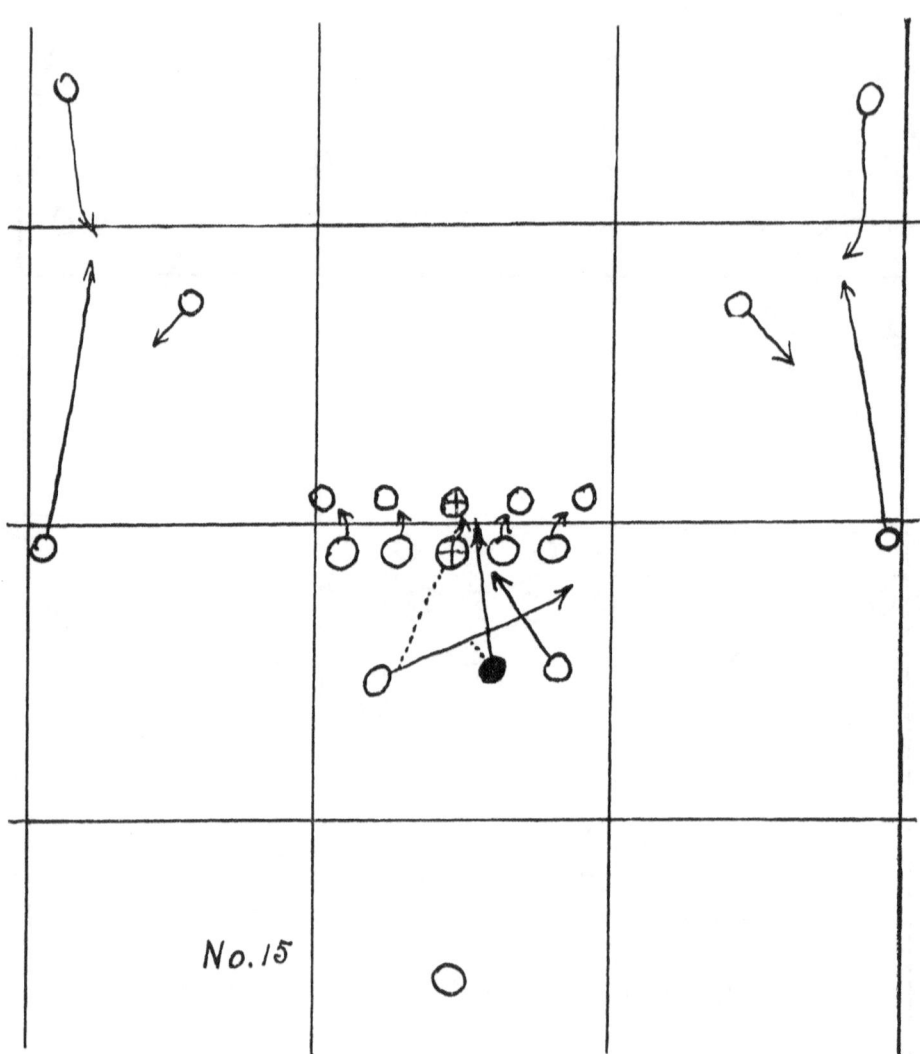

No. 15

No. 15.—Fake kick through a quick opening in the line. The ball is passed to left half, who runs with it as though to go around the opposing left tackle, but hands it to th player indicated in the diagram, who goes through center and guard with right half pushing him. Center and right guard make an opening.

1908 Offense 31

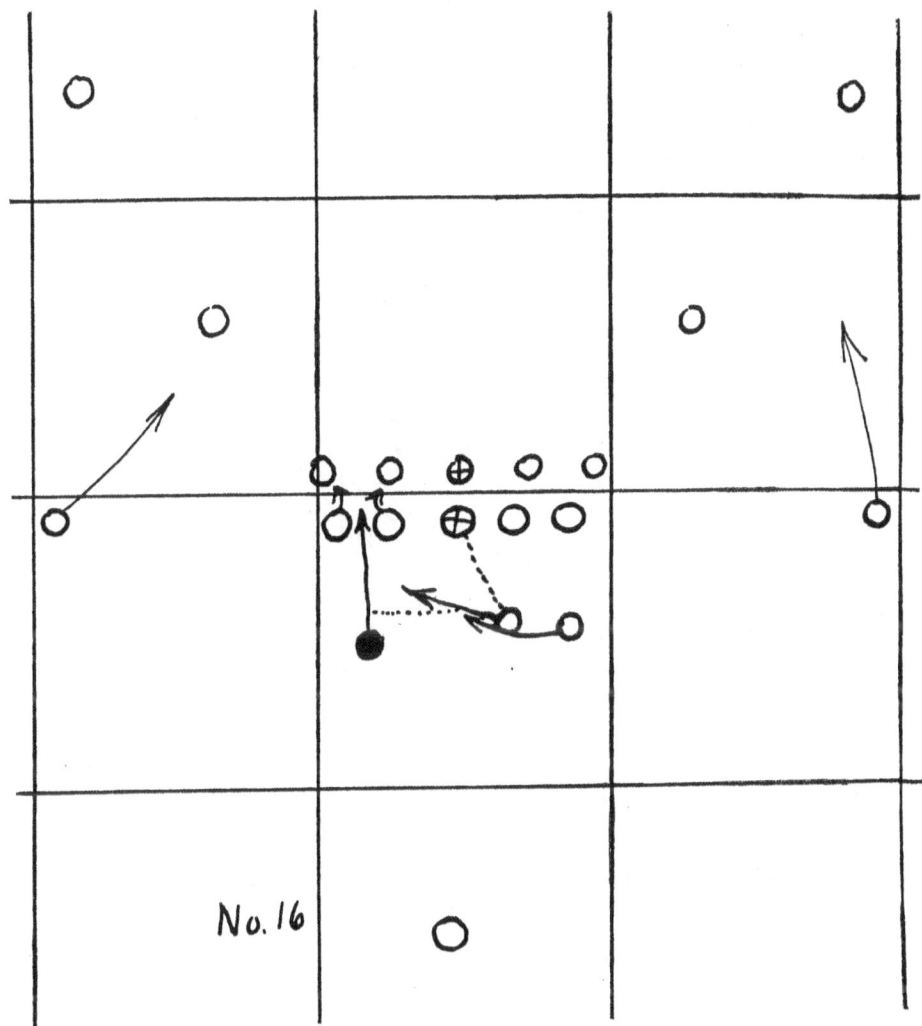

No. 16

No. 16.—Fake kick. The ball is passed to quarter and he passes it across to left half, who darts through the line between guard and tackle. Quarter and right half tandem through with him, so that the play will gain whether an opening is made or not, because of the push behind it.

1908 Offense

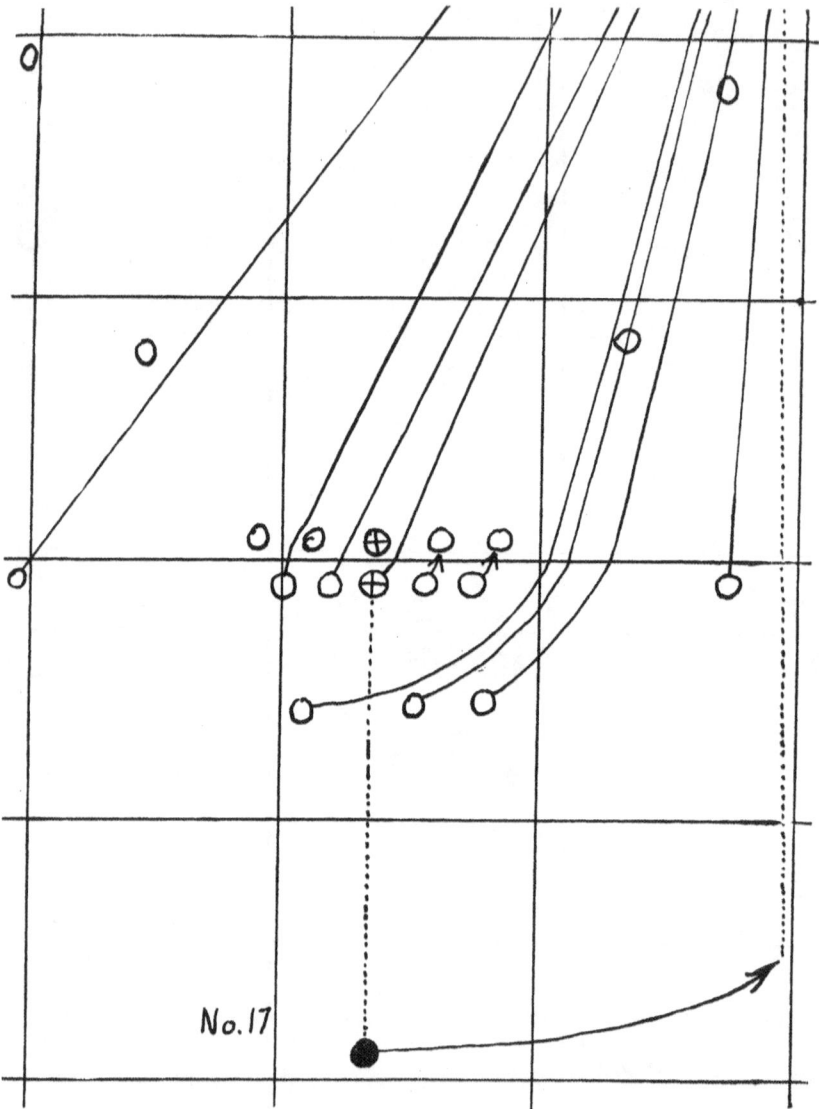

No. 17.—This is the long forward pass play used so successfully last season. Right guard and tackle block their men so as to allow the backs to pass by. The other men go down the field at once. Left end and tackle are assigned the special duty of blocking the back field man who is on their side (when there are two men back to receive the punt or pass). Left guard and center should put the other back out, while the three backs and end string out down the field, so that one of them is sure to be near the spot where the ball is thrown. When one of them is sure he can get under the ball he yells "I have it," and the others protect him by blocking off opponents. Under the new rules only the man who has touched the ball can secure it if it is fumbled, unless it has touched an opponent.

1908 Offense 33

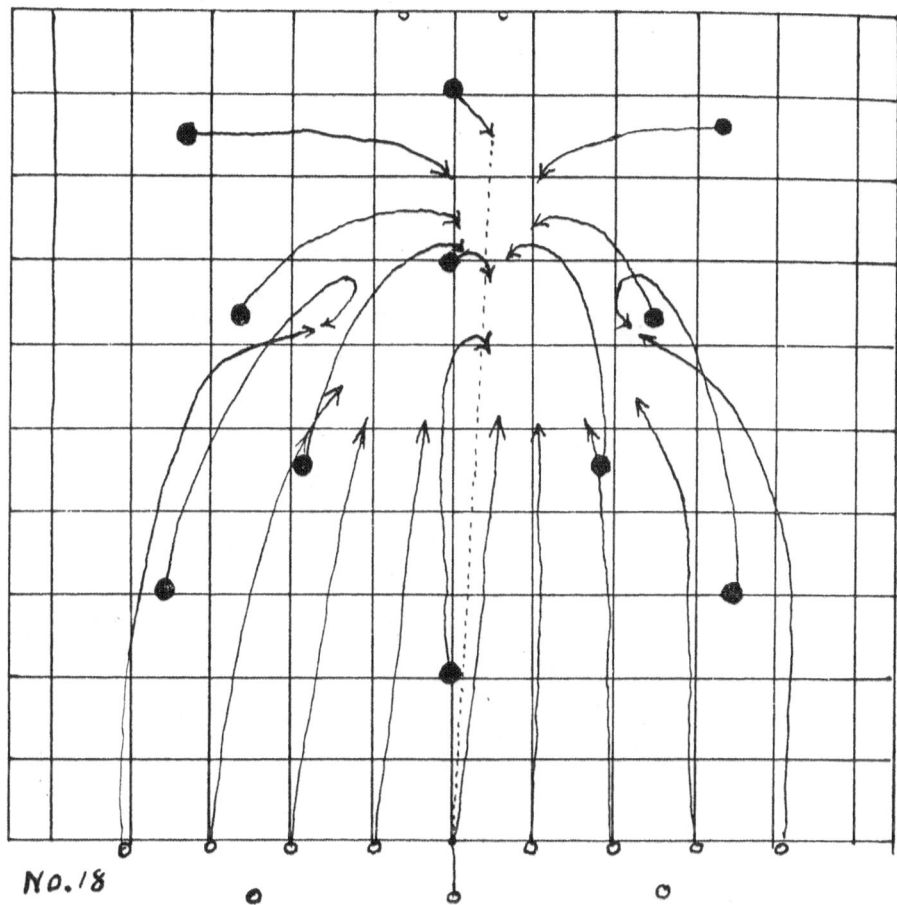

No. 18

No. 18.—This diagram explains a good formation and interference for running back kick-offs, kick-outs from the the twenty five yard line, and place kicks (after fair catches) which do not score or result in touchbacks.

The ends should be fifteen yards from the side line, so as to guard against short kicks to the side. Center stands ten yards from the ball, also to guard against a short kick. The diagram shows positions of all. The distance the backs should stand from the ball depends upon the wind, and upon the ability of the kicker. The whole team should run back toward the spot where the ball is to be caught, and turn in time to block opponents and form fast and close interference for the runner. The ends should keep on the inside of their opponents, and block them out as they turn in to tackle the runner. In fact all the men should endeavor to block their opponents out. Center should dodge the ball if kicked low, because if it hits him his opponents are more likely to get it than he.

On kick-outs the formation is the same, except that center stands on the twenty-five yard line and tries to block the kick.

1908 Offense

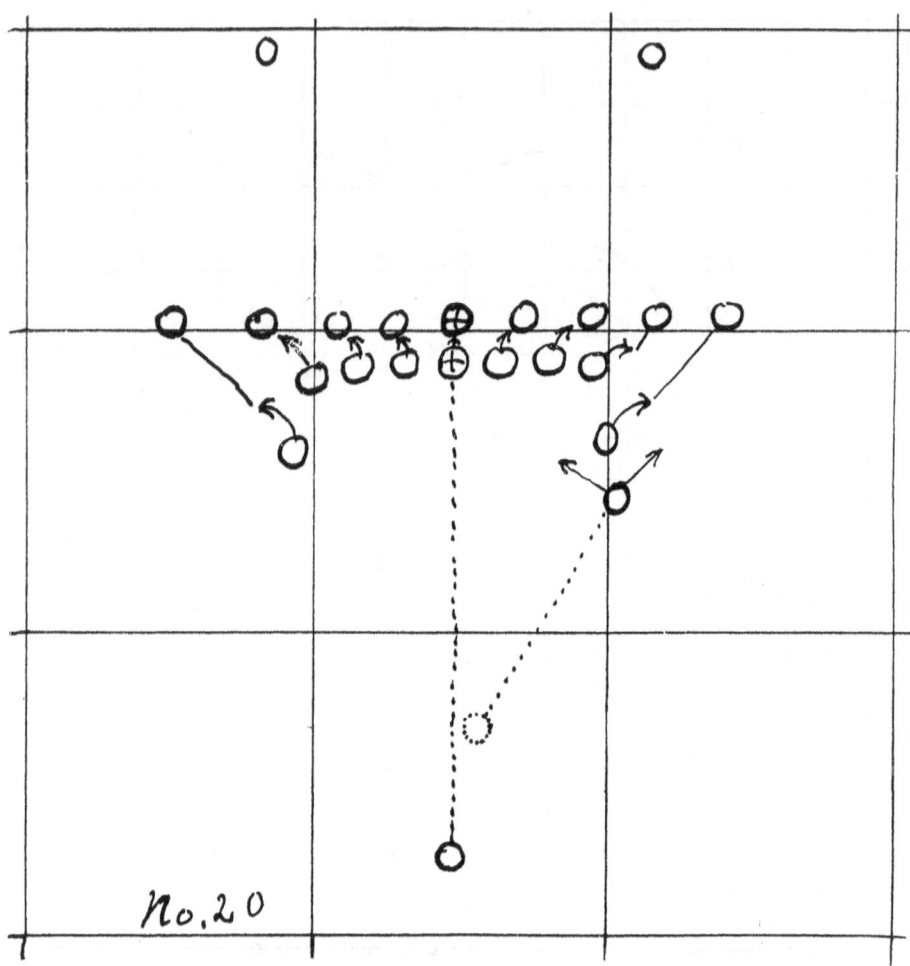

No. 20.—Drop-kick or quick place-kick formation. Solid circles show formation for a drop-kick, and the dotted circle shows the holder of the ball and where he should be, in case the trial is to be by a quick place-kick. Every man who is protecting the kicker (excepting the center) should make it a point to block his man outward, so that if his opponent breaks through it will be difficult for him to get in front of the ball. In case of the drop-kick, the extra back on the right should watch for and block any man coming through the center.

1908 Offense 35

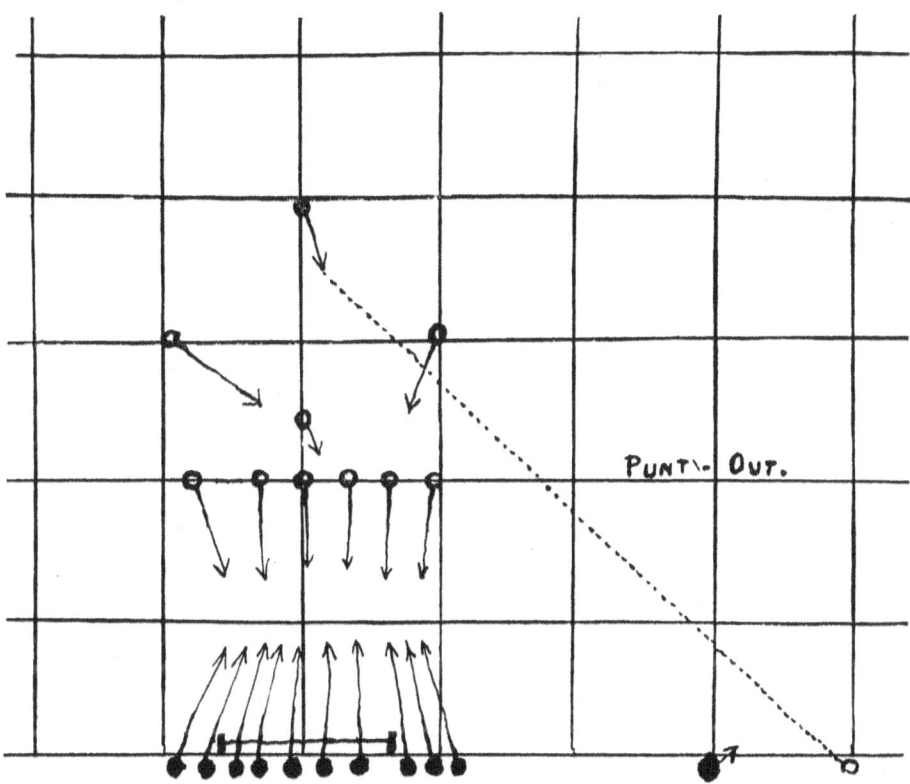

PUNT-OUT.—A punt-out should be made after a touchdown in case the ball is declared dead more than ten yards to either side of the goal, and the diagram shows how the two teams should line up. There should be four of the best punt catchers of the punter's side stationed so as to cover the ground where the punt is likely to fall, and when one of them is sure he can catch the ball he should yell "I have it," and all the rest of his team should advance toward the opponents, so as to block them and protect the catcher

A COURSE IN FOOTBALL FOR PLAYERS AND COACHES

OFFENSE

Supplement

Copyright unknown but likely 1909

GLENN S. WARNER, ATHLETIC DIRECTOR
INDIAN SCHOOL, CARLISLE, PENNA.

Offense

SUPPLEMENT

It will be a good plan for every team to have an on-side kick or two as well as several forward pass plays so that on wet days, when the ball is slippery and hard to handle, the on side kicks can be used to advantage while the forward pass plays will be found to work better on dry days. Both can be used to advantage in any kind of weather, but experience has proved that, as a rule, the on-side kick is more adapted to wet weather conditions than the forward pass.

The plays that have been diagrammed can be changed slightly without weakening them, when another player, other than the one indicated in the diagrams, is better suited to make the play. For instance, in play No. 7, the end or front man in the tamdem can carry the ball just as effectively as the full-back, and if the end is good at bucking the line, he can be used in this play very effectively. If the tackle is a good man carrying the ball he can do so with very good interference as shown in plays Nos. 3 and 9. The left half would then keep on the tackle's outside and help turn him as he passes the opposing tackle.

Another strong tamden play would be to shove the end or front man in the tandem, through the center in the same manner as No. 7 is played, with the exception that the left tackle would then block his man instead of coming back to push, while the right half would then block his man instead of coming back to push, while the right half would push on the play instead of going through to block as in No. 7.

Following are some diagrams and explanations of plays from the end back formation which will be found to be very effective if worked up and played correctly.

1909 Supplement 39

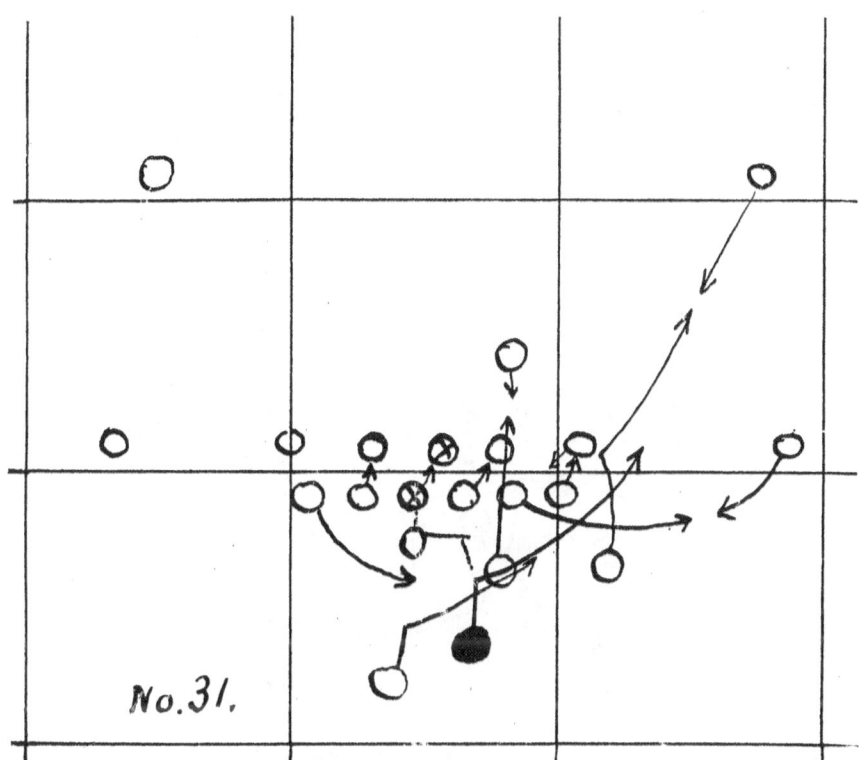

No. 31.

No. 31. This is a fake play but with just enough push behind it to make it a good ground gainer even if the fake does not fool any of the opponents. The play starts off exactly like No. 7, the end or first man making a bluff to take the ball from the quarter. The full back takes one step forward with his left foot, receives the ball from the quarter, and then shoots outside of tackle. Left half takes one step in the same manner and then goes with the full back, pushing him from the rear. Quarter and left tackle also get behind and push. Right tackle leaves his position on the snap of the ball and goes out and blocks the opposing end, while right half back helps the opposing tackle out of the way and blocks the half-back. This play will work for good gains if played in this way provided the opposing end is playing wide enough so that the right tackle can block him a moment. If the opposing end is playing very close to his tackle, then the right half-back must block the end out and right tackle will hold his position in the line.

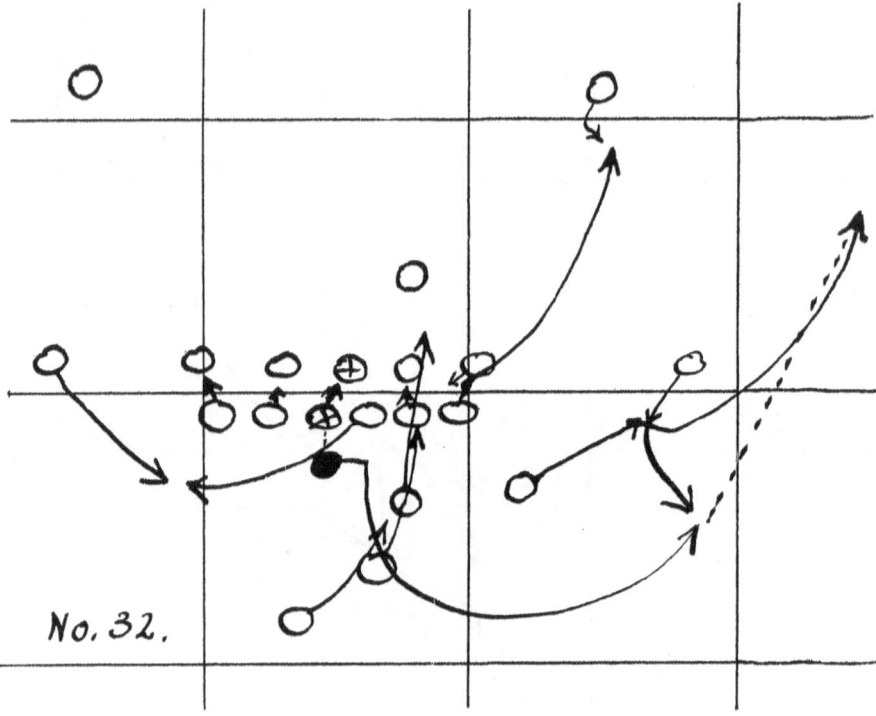

No. 32.

No. 32. This play is much the same as No. 11, except that the quarter runs with the ball after faking to give it to one of the men in the tandem, and when he has run as far as he can he passes the ball forward to right half, who blocks the end and then keeps about ten yards in front of the quarter, ready to receive the pass. Right end goes out to protect the right half. If the opposing right end is playing close in, and liable to catch the quarter from behind, the right guard leaves his position with the snap of the ball and goes out and blocks the end as shown in the diagram. If the end is playing wide and not following up the plays fast, then the guard need not leave his position. This play is really an improvement on No. 11 and will be found a very good one.

1909 Supplement 41

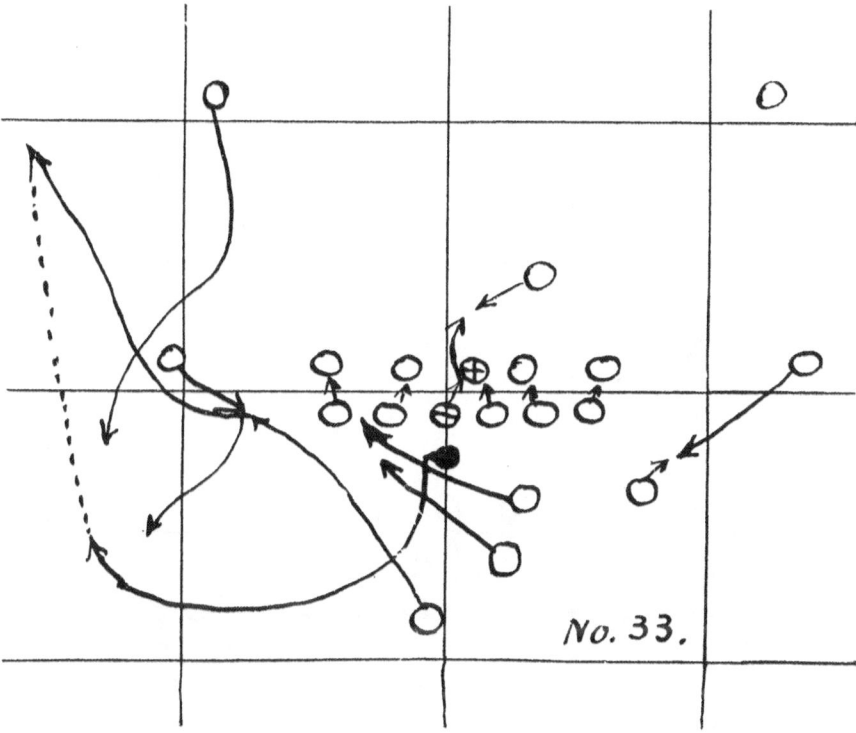

No. 33.

No. 33. This play starts off like No. 8. The quarter fakes to pass the ball to the end, full back pushes the end through the line, while the left half goes for the opposing end. After faking, the quarter swings around and the primary object of the play should be to gain by a quarter-back run, If however, the left half is unable to block the opposing end, he continues on and is ready to receive a forward pass from the quarter as soon as the latter is about to be tackled, This is an excellent play and is very effective because it is played to the short side. If the opponents left end is playing close to tackle and likely to catch the quarter from behind, the right half holds his ground and blocks, but if there is no danger of any one from the rear, the right half can get into the play. either ahead of the quarter to interfere, or following up to push or aid in any other way.

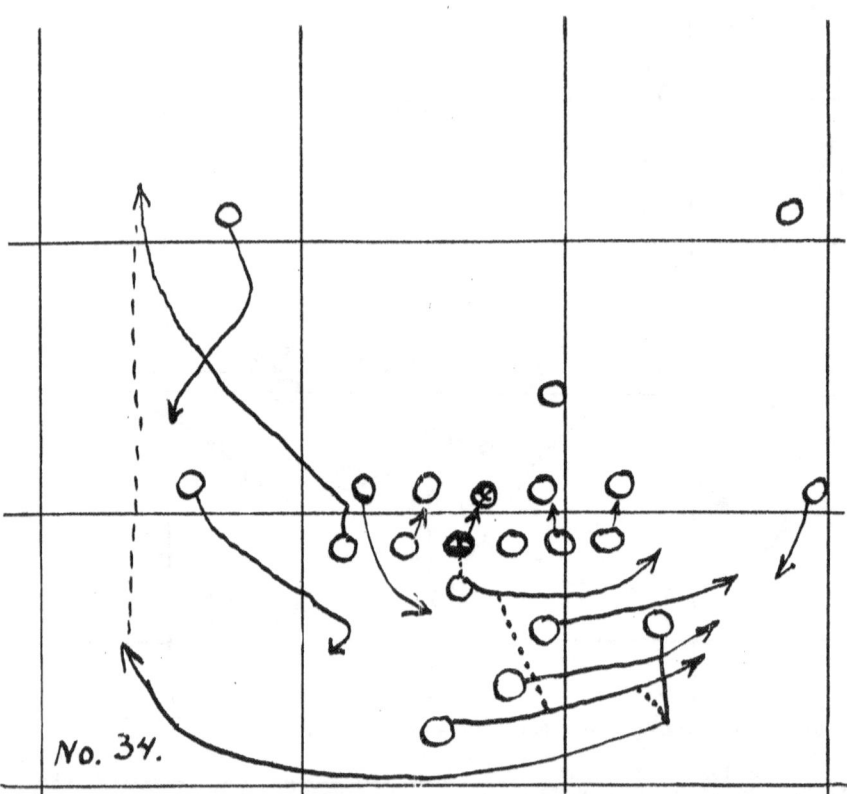

No. 34. This play is made to look like No. 9. All the men behind the line excepting right half start for the end. Right half backs up, keeping low down and out of sight as much as possible, and receives the ball from the left half. He should not start until he receives the ball and then he should swing back of the runner pretty well, so as not to be intercepted by players who are chasing up the play from behind. The primary object of this play should be to gain ground by the run. The left tackle moves out and always keeps ten yards ahead of the runner so as to receive the forward pass when the runner has gone as far as he can. This provides another play around the short side.

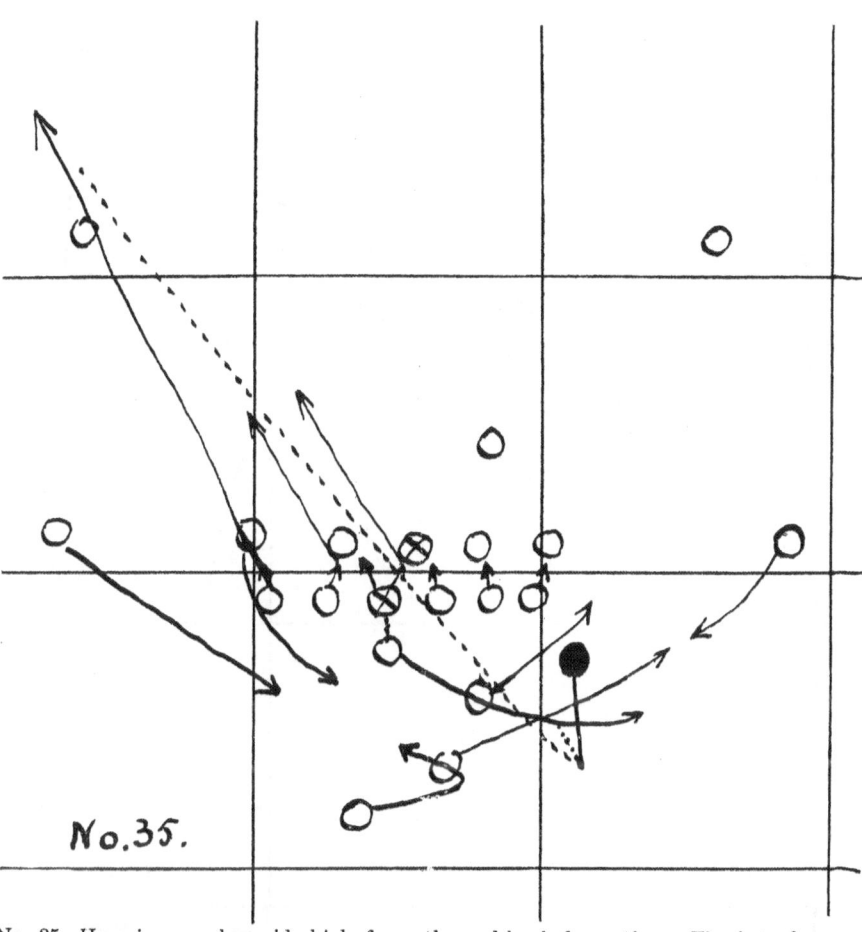

No. 35.

No. 35. Here is a good on side kick from the end-back formation. The interference starts off to the right but left half stops and blocks the opposing right tackle or end. Right half backs up and receives the ball from the quarter as he passes him and then kicks the ball to the left. Left tackle goes down fast to get the ball as soon as it touches the ground. The other linemen also go down after blocking. This play is being used successfully by the Indians and, while it is impossible to get the ball every time, it is proving a great play to use on third down and can be worked as a short kick when near the opponent's goal or as a long surprise kick to kick over the heads of the opposing quarter when near the center of the field.

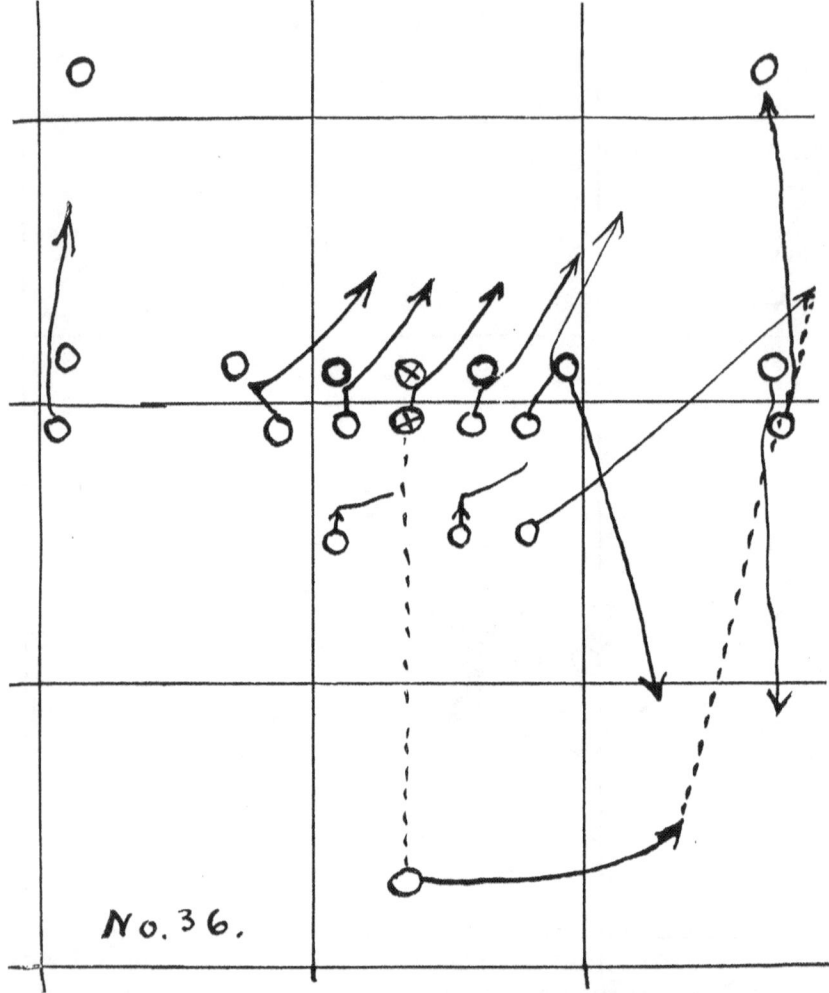

No. 36. The long forward pass is more difficult to make than a short one and the chances of making it work are less than a shorter one as the changes in the rules have crippled the play to a certain extent. The long pass No. 17 is still a good one and when successfully made results in a big gain, but it may be found more advantageous to use a shorter pass from the punt formation, and certainly the short pass will be a good one to mix in with the long pass and the end run (No. 13). In this play the line-men block as they would for a punt. Left half and the other back who is protecting the punter, also stand still and block. Right end blocks the half back who is in front of him or the opposing end, if the latter is playing back. In that case the right tackle goes through and blocks the back. If the opposing end or a back is on the line he will be drawn in when the punter starts to run with the ball. Right half runs out about seven yards or more from center and about two or three yards across the scrimmage line and receives the pass from the supposed punter, who first starts to run with it and then passes forward. The other line men work over in front of the right half, after blocking, so as to interfere for him after he has secured the ball. This will work nearly every time for fairly good gains and sometimes for a long run.

A COURSE IN FOOTBALL FOR PLAYERS AND COACHES

OFFENSE

Copyright unknown but likely 1910

GLENN S. WARNER, ATHLETIC DIRECTOR
INDIAN SCHOOL, CARLISLE, PENNA.

This shows correct positions of the players upon regular formation ready for the ball to be snapped, except that the quarter should have his hands extended toward the ball, instead of upon his knees.

Offense

EVERY team's offense should consist of a limited number of first class plays, perfectly mastered, and of sufficient variety to enable it to meet any style of defense under all sorts of conditions, and be able to take advantage of any weakness which might develop in the defense of opposing teams. No team should depend upon one style of attack. The offensive strength should consist of straight, powerful line plays, end runs with perfectly formed interference, two or three fake plays which have some power in them, and do not depend entirely upon deceiving the opponents, two or three good forward pass plays, and several plays from the punt formation. These should be combined with ability to kick field goals, and an onside kick or two might be of value, although the forward pass can easily be made to serve for the latter.

Under the new rules the tendency will be to do away with the quarter-back passing the ball and the ball will be passed by most teams directly from center to runner. There will also be a tendency to use more open formation plays because, not being permitted to push or pull, the backs must now go ahead of the runner and form protection for him and open up a passage through the line as well as around the ends. The forward pass will be more used than in the past few years, because of the removal of some of its restrictions, protecting the receiver of it, and lessening the penalty when it is not properly played.

Many teams are unwisely taught a large number of plays—so many that it is impossible to master them all thoroughly, and often resulting in confusion of signals. It is much better to have a few good plays well learned, than to have a large assortment imperfectly worked up and some of which are likely to be of doubtful strength. The more important and harder the game the fewer plays are used, because the team has the ball less, has to punt more, and when rushing the ball only uses a select few of its strongest plays.

Trick plays are useful to add variety to the attack, to keep the opponents guessing and thus aid the regular plays, and occasionally to pull off a long run, but they should not be depended upon to win games, and only a few good ones should be taught the players.

In diagraming the following plays, care has been taken to select only those which are sure to be good ones. Many more might be explained, but the list here diagramed is large enough, and varied enough, to enable any team to select from it a powerful, scientific and varied attack, which will succeed against the defense of any team in its class.

The plays are diagramed upon five yard squares, so that the approximate distance can be seen at a glance, and each play is only diagramed for one side of the line. How the same play should be played on the opposite side, can easily be figured out by studying the diagrams, or by copying the plays upon a thin sheet of paper, holding to the light, and looking at the reverse side. The man who carries the ball is indicated by the solid black circle. The defensive back, who plays in the extreme back-field to handle punts, etc., is not shown in the diagrams.

There are eight plays diagramed for one side of the line from the regular formation, or sixteen in all; eight diagrams, or sixteen plays from the backs-over formation; five diagrams, or ten plays from the open formation; and six diagrams or twelve plays from the punt formation. This furnishes a total of fifty-four selected plays, without counting the punt, drop-kick, or quick place-kick. Twenty good plays are enough for any team, and no team should have over twenty-five.

The regular simple formation plays and the punts should be given the team as early as possible, and the forward passes and other plays should then be mastered at the rate of about two or three each week.

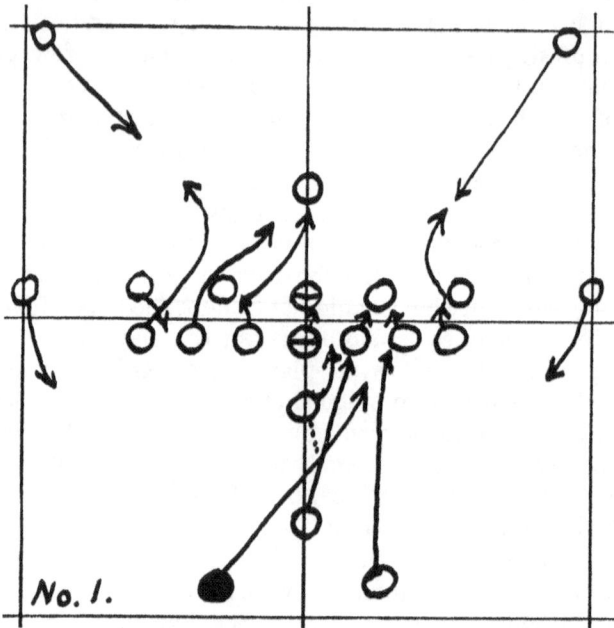

No. 1. This play is designed to go through the opposing guard, or between him and the tackle. Quarter passes the ball to left half-back who carries the ball as indicated behind interference formed by the fullback and right half-back. The guard and tackle carry the opposing guard back and to the left, while the right end throws the opposing tackle out. If the opposing guard plays close to his center so that the guard can handle him alone the tackle can then aid the end in disposing of the opposing tackle. The quarter advances into the line as indicated to help bend the line back. All the line men should go through and block the secondary defense after first putting their opposing linemen out of the play.

1910 Offense

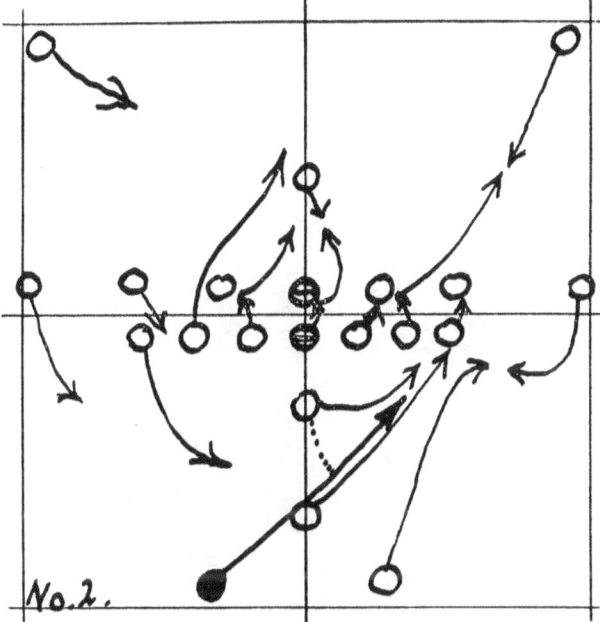

No. 2. This is a mass upon tackle or a straight-off-tackle play. Left half-back takes the ball behind the quarter, full-back and right half-back. The play should be aimed just outside your own right end. Right half runs shoulder to shoulder with his full-back and then dives into the opposing end and throws him out just as he comes in to tackle. Right half should not run out and toward the end, but close in as indicated, so that he will be sure to be in position to block the end out. If the opposing left guard is playing wide the tackle will have to help his guard take care of him, but if he is playing close to center the tackle can help his end put the opposing tackle out of the play and go through to block the secondary defense. Left end comes around to make the play safe.

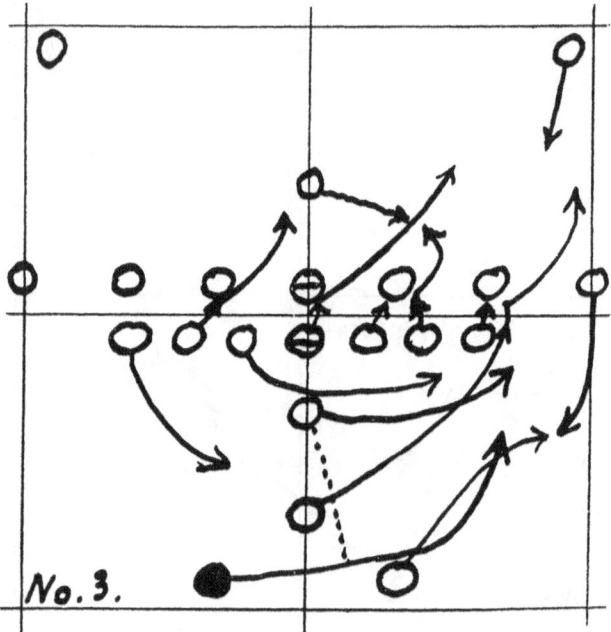

No. 3. Short end run aimed to go between opposing tackle and end. In this play the left half should start as for a wide end run so as to allow his interference plenty of time to form and to bring the opposing end pretty well out, so that right half can block him out just as the runner turns in. Full back helps the end block the opposing tackle and then blocks defensive left half. Right tackle helps the guard if his opponent plays very wide, otherwise he helps his end block the tackle. Left guard and quarter get into the interference, and left end follows up the play to guard against a fumble and to keep opponents from tackling from behind. Other linemen block as indicated and go through to cut off the secondry defense.

1910 Offense

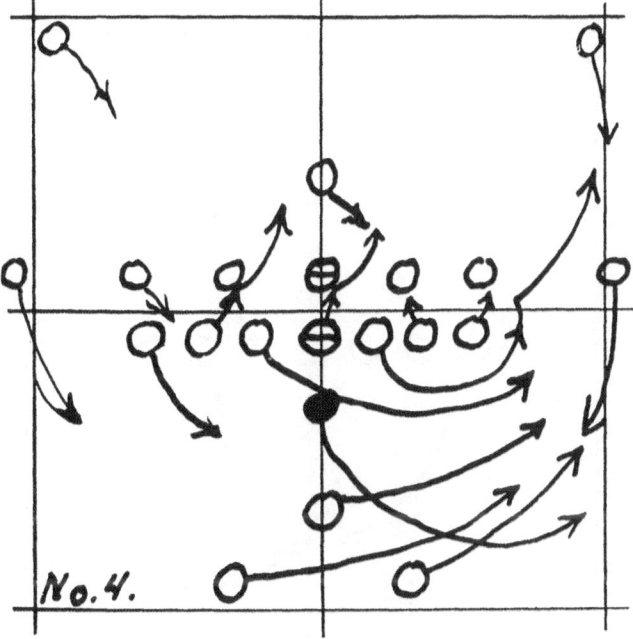

No. 4. Wide quarter back run. In this play both full back and right half should dispose of the opposing left end, and left half should also take him if he eludes the other interference. Both guards can get into the interference in this play and they are an important factor in its success. The quarter starts pretty well back and should get off with a lot of speed being careful not to run too close to the line. After he gets started he should look for openings and turn straight down the field as soon as an opening presents itself. Left end comes around to look after fumbles and to protect the runner from behind.

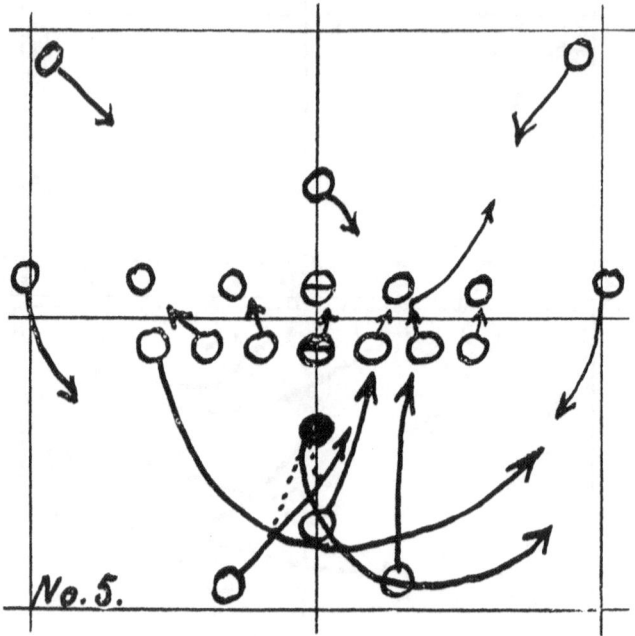

No. 5. This is a fake line attack and double pass quarter-back run. The play starts off exactly as No. 1. Quarter passes the ball to left half and stands with his back to the center. Left half hands quarter the ball as he passes him and the quarter starts pretty wide, coming out behind his left end, who leaves his position with the snap of the ball and comes around as interference for the quarter, putting the opposing left end out of the play. Left tackle helps block momentarily and then goes through and blocks defensive left half. This is an excellent play with a fast quarter if properly played and made to look like No. 1 when it starts off.

1910 Offense

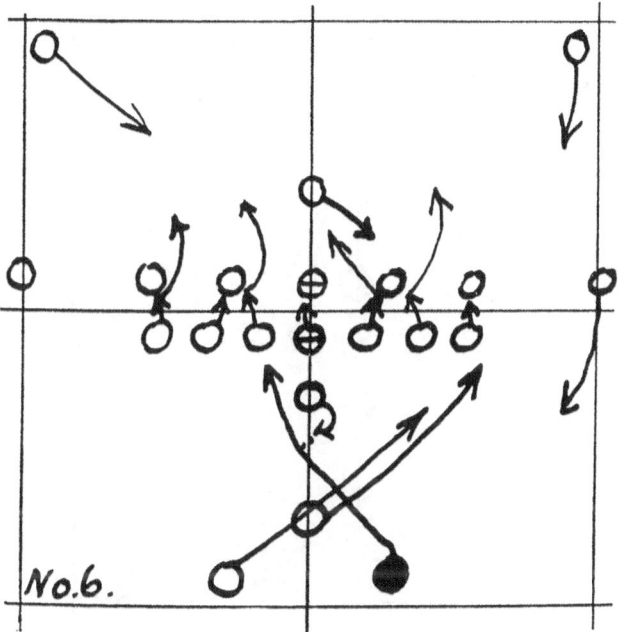

No. 6. This is a delayed pass which works well. The play is made to look like No. 2. The left half makes a bluff to take the ball from the quarter who turns to the right and makes a fake pass to him. Right half lays low, perhaps taking one step to the right, and then shoots to the left as the other backs have passed. The hole should be made either between guard and center, or guard and tackle, whichever works best, and the right half should be on the alert to take the opening wherever it is.

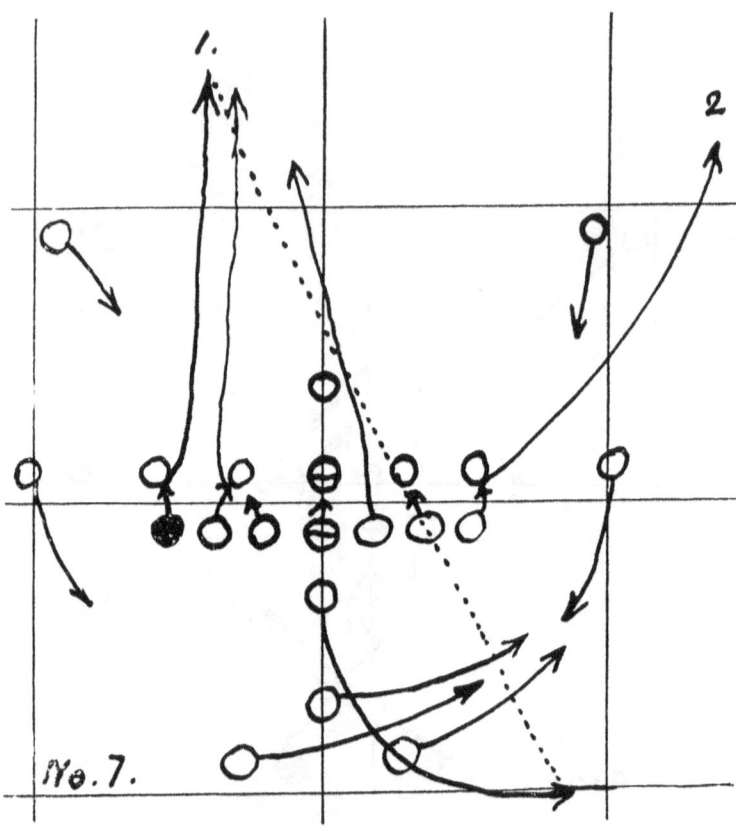

No. 7. Forward pass. This play starts off as a quarter-back run similar to No. 4, except that the linemen do not get into the interference. Quarter comes back and runs wide and far enough to allow his left end to get well down the field. He then passes the ball to left end if the latter is free, but he can also pass to right end, or continue running with the ball if both ends are covered. It may work better for the left end to run farther out to the left in this play, and the quarter must remember to run far enough back so that the pass is made at least five yards behind the line.

1910 Offense

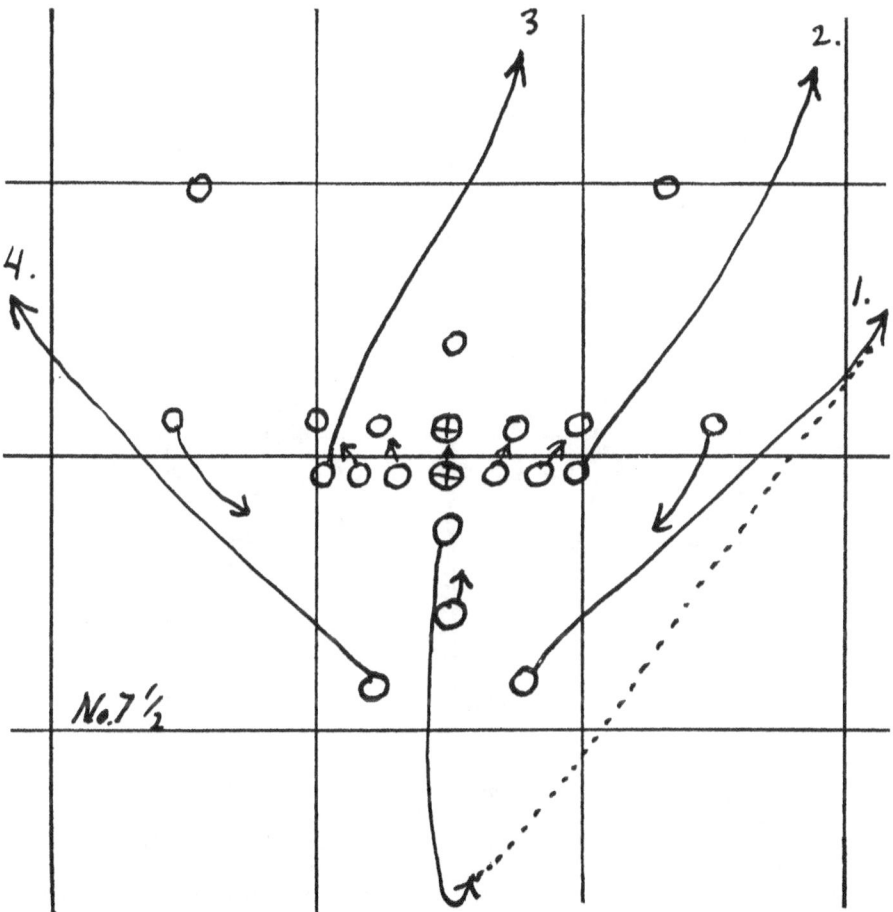

No. 7½. An excellent forward pass. Players numbered 1, 2, 3, and 4 run quickly upon the snap of the ball as indicated. Fullback holds his position and protects quarter back who gets the ball from center and runs quickly back from five to ten yards and then turns and passes the ball to No. 1, 2, 3, or 4. Probably the pass will work better to No. 1, because the secondary defense will very likely be drawn away from him to cover No. 2 and 3. The latter players should look around and be ready in case the ball is thrown to either of them. If opposing left end follows No. 1, out the quarter can continue running to the right until the end comes after him.

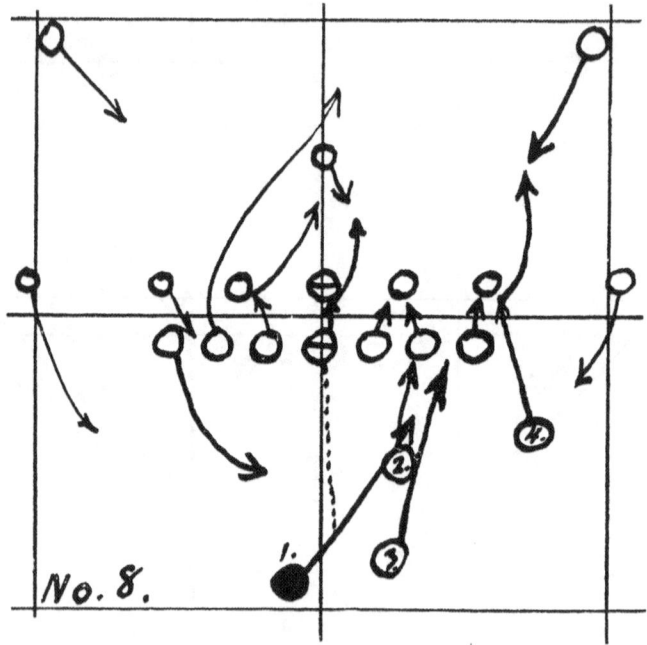

No. 8. This play and those following up to No. 16, are from a direct pass formation in which the backs are massed upon one side of the ball. Left half stands back about four and a half to five yards from the line and behind the hole between his left guard and center. No. 3 stands slightly closer to the line and back of right guard. No. 2 stands about two and a half yards back of the line and behind the opening between right guard and right tackle. No. 4 stands outside of his right end and about a yard and a half to two yards back but he can move closer or up to the line if the opposing tackle plays very wide so that right end has trouble in blocking him.

In this play left half takes the ball on a direct pass and carries it behind Nos. 2 and 3 between the opposing left guard and tackle, No. 4 helps block tackle and goes on to cut off defensive left half. Left end comes around to make the play safe.

1910 Offense

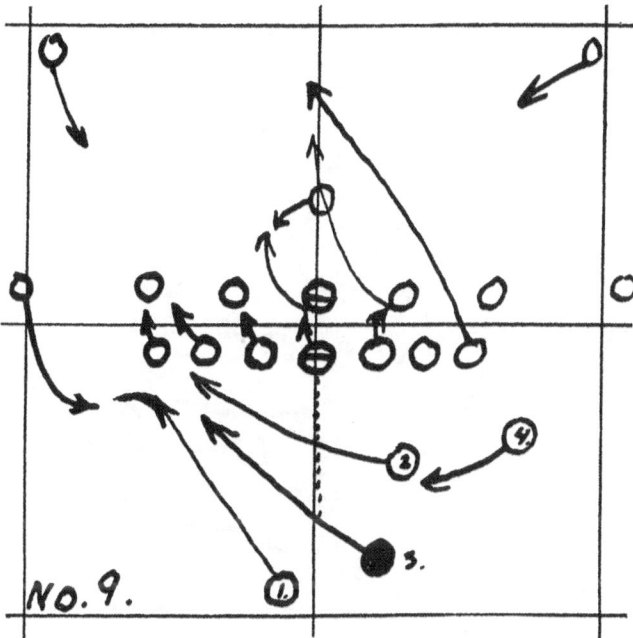

No. 9. This is a play to the weak side just off tackle. No. 5 takes the ball on a direct pass with Nos. 2 and 1 to interfere for him. No. 1 runs close in and then dives into and forces the defensive end out as he comes in to tackle. No. 4 makes the play safe and the line men block or go through to cut off secondary defense as indicated.

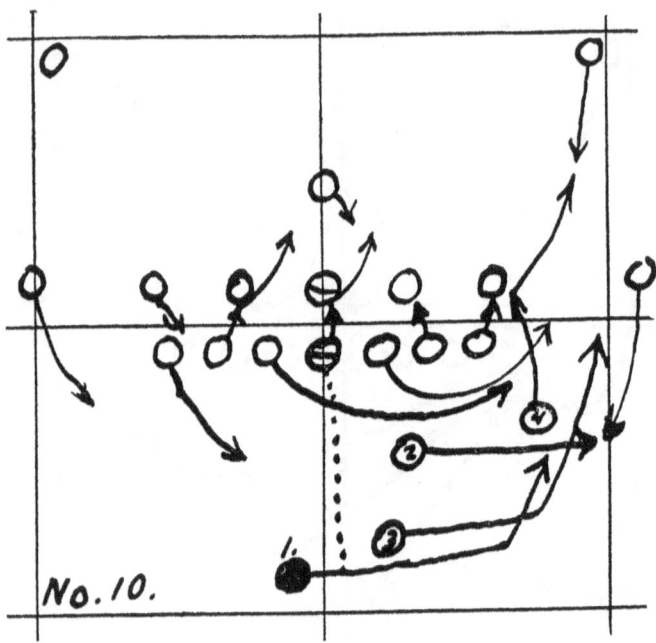

No. 10. Short end run. No. 2 blocks the defensive end out. No. 4 helps block the defensive tackle and then takes the defensive half. No. 1 carries the ball and follows No. 3 running wide for three or four yards as if to circle the end and then cutting in quickly as No. 2 blocks the end out. Both guards leave their positions with the snap of the ball and come around in the interference in which they form an effective part. Left tackle and center block as indicated and then go through to cut off secondary defense. Left end follows up the play to recover possible fumble and to protect the runner from behind. This is a very effective ground gainer.

1910 Offense

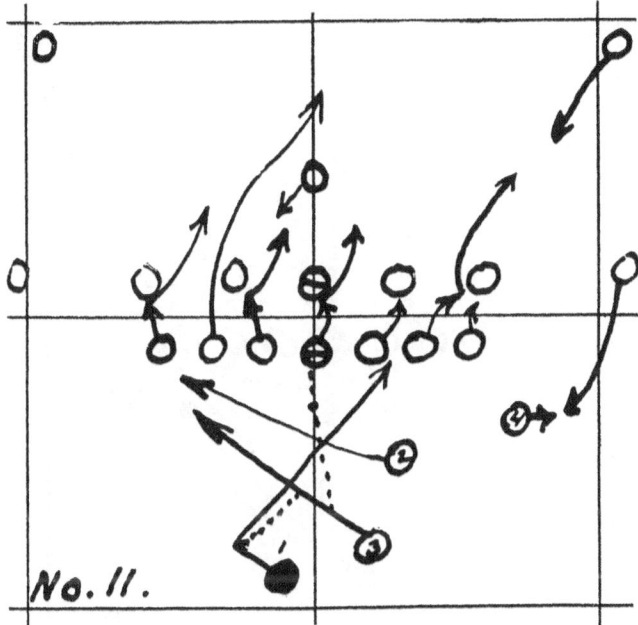

No. 11. Fake tackle play and delayed pass. This play is made to look like No. 9. No. 3 taking the ball and passing to No. 1 as he passes him. No. 1 takes one step with his left foot, keeping close to the ground and, after securing the ball, carries it between opponent's left guard and left tackle. No. 1 should be careful not to run from his position but take one step to the left, stop, get the ball and then run from that point. The taking of but one step and then a complete stop is necessary to enable the back to turn sharply before getting too close to the line.

1910 Offense

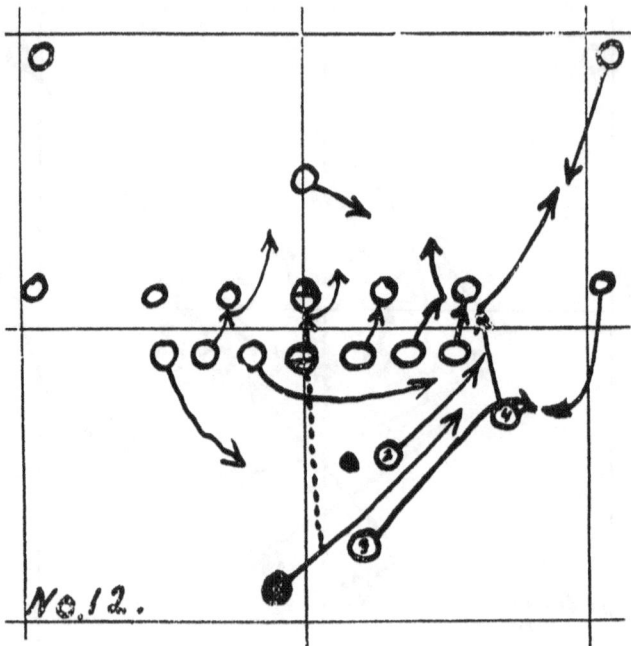

No. 12. Mass upon tackle. This play is aimed to just slide off the opposing tackle. No. 4 helps drive the tackle back and then blocks defensive half. No 1 takes the ball behind No. 2, and left guard protects him from the side. No. 3 runs close to No. 2 so as to be sure to be inside the defensive end and then blocks the latter out as he comes in to tackle the runner.

1910 Offense 61

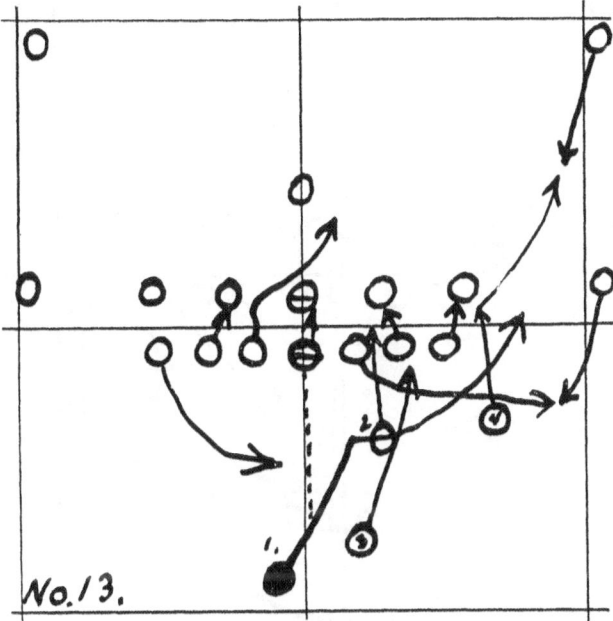

No. 13. This play starts off and is made to look like No. 8. The right guard leaves his position with the snap of the ball and goes out to block the defensive end. Coming from so close to the line the latter will not notice him until too late. No. 2 shoots into the hole left vacant by the guard. No. 3 runs for the hole the other side of his right tackle. No. 1 takes the ball and advances two or three short steps slightly to the right of center and then turns sharply and speedily to the right, just going outside of tackle. This is a very deceiving and effective play if played properly. No. 1 should be careful not to start too fast so that he cannot turn quickly before getting too close to the line.

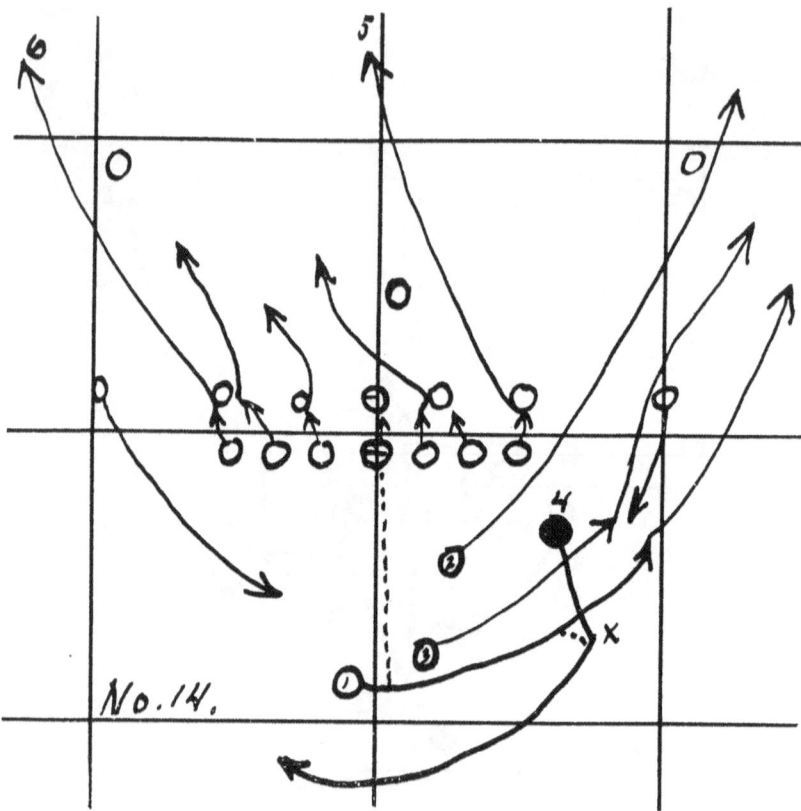

No. 14. Criss-cross forward pass or run. No. 4 backs up, keeping low and not starting to run until he secures the ball from No. 1 who runs with it as though for a run around right end. As No. 1 passes No. 4 he places the ball against the latter's stomach. No. 4 should at that time be at X and facing in the direction he is to run. He should run well back and to the left, after securing the ball, and if he sees that the opponent's right end has overrun him he can continue the play as a run. If he sees that he is likely to be intercepted he can pass the ball to No. 6, No. 5, or across to No. 1, 2 or 3. Probably No. 6 will be best man to pass to. The runner must run far enough back so as to elude opposing right end and to have time to make the pass at least five yards back of the line.

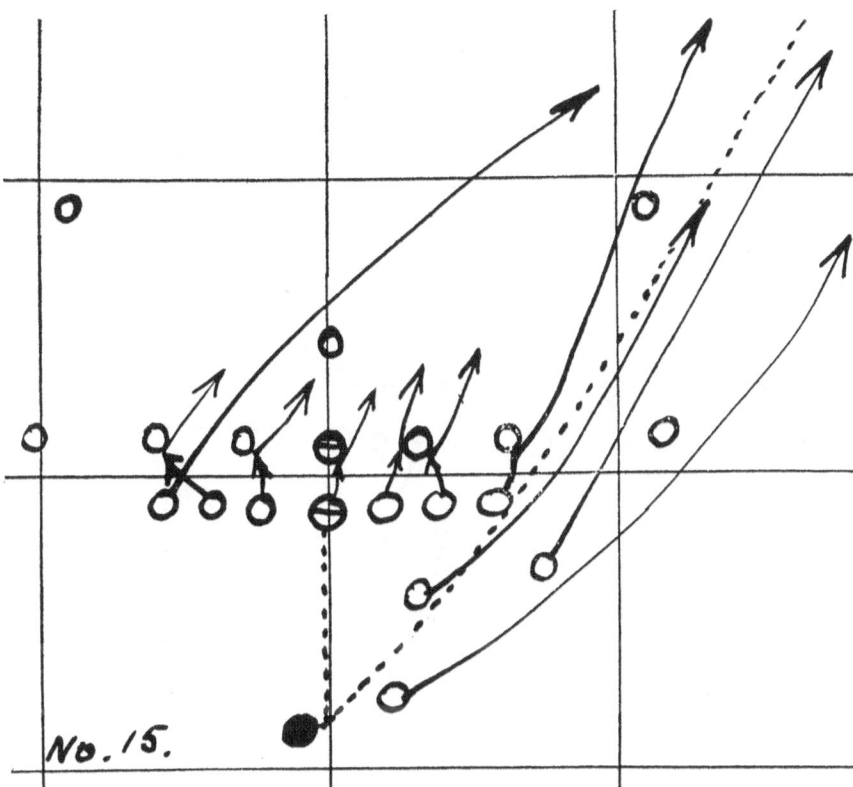

No. 15. This is a quick punt which can be used as an onside kick or for the purpose of punting over the defensive full back's head if he comes up closer to the scrimmage line than he should. The ends and backs charge down the field with the snap of the ball. The punter can step back a yard or two while recovering the ball from center or he can start to run with it a few steps before punting. This makes the play more effective because it gives the ends and backs more time to get down the field and it also takes more time for the defense to diagnose the play.

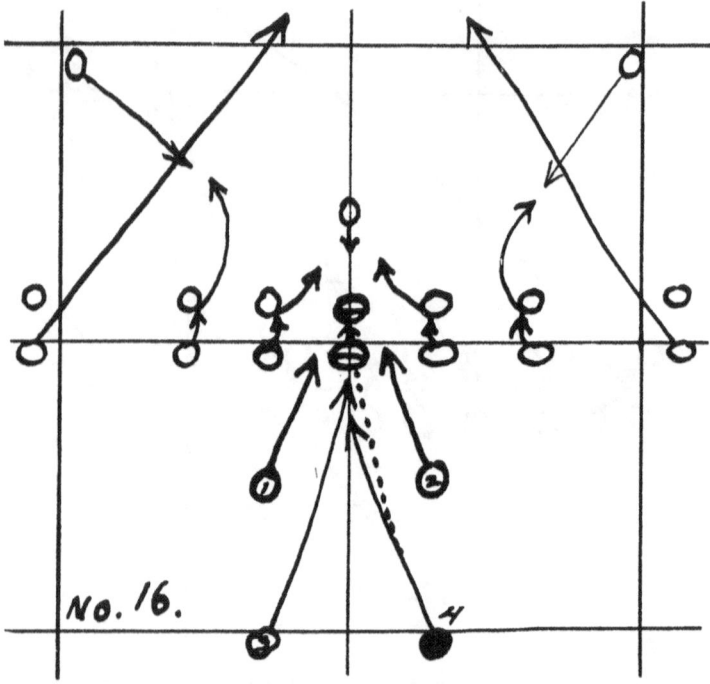

No. 16. This play and the following up to No. 21, are from an open formation which will prove very effective under the new rules. The linemen all play opposite their opponents and, as the defense is usually pretty well spread out, the result will be a very open formation. Two of the backs play about three yards back of the line and about three yards apart. The other two backs play about six yards from the line and the same distance apart, the four backs forming a square. In this position either of the two backs numbered 3 and 4 can attack any spot in the line with the other three backs for interference, thus forming mass plays as well as end runs without violating the rules. The open line tends to prevent congestion when the play hits the line. This play is an attack upon center which explains itself. Nos. 1, 2 and 3 interfere for No. 4. Guards and tackles block their men out and then go through and block off the secondary defense as indicated. The ends go down the field at once so as to interfere for the runner if he gets through the line.

From this formation the center can pass the ball to either No. 1 or No. 2, for dashes through quick openings in the line between guard and tackle when a short gain is needed.

1910 Offense

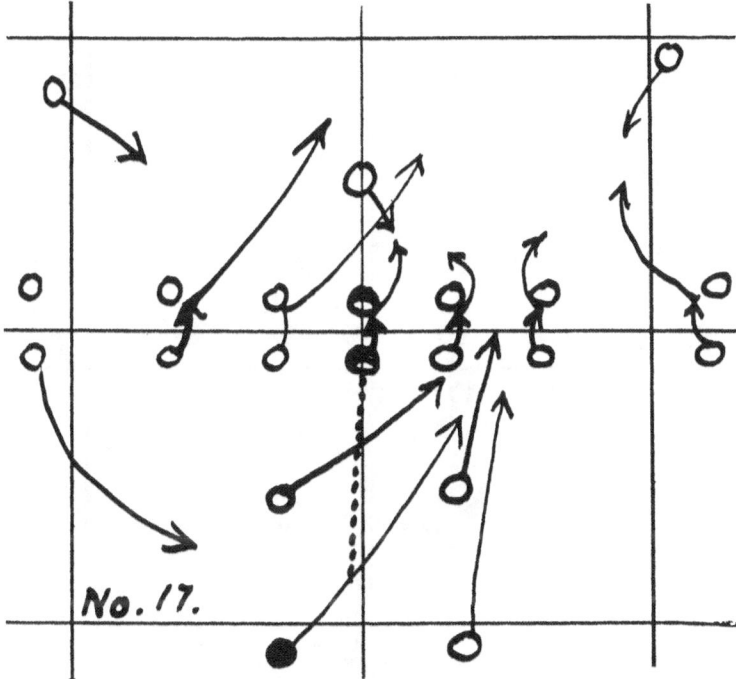

No. 17. This play is very similar to the preceeding play except that it is aimed between guard and tackle. Left end comes around to guard against opponents securing the ball upon a fumble and to protect the runner from the rear.

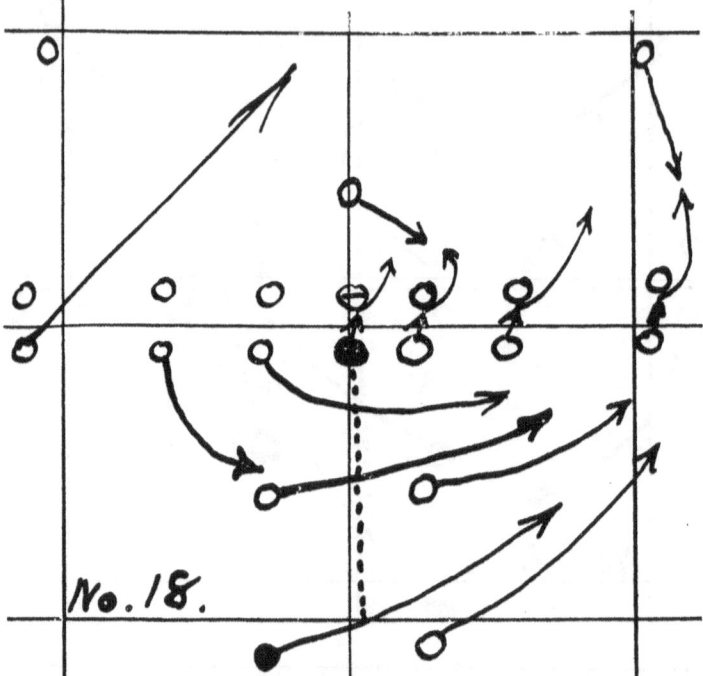

No. 18. End run. Left half takes the ball around right end, the other backs and left guard interfering for him. Left tackle follows up the play and makes it safe, while left end cuts across the field to interfere for the runner if he gets by the line. Center and the right side of the line block long and hard and then go through and cut off secondary defense.

1910 Offense 67

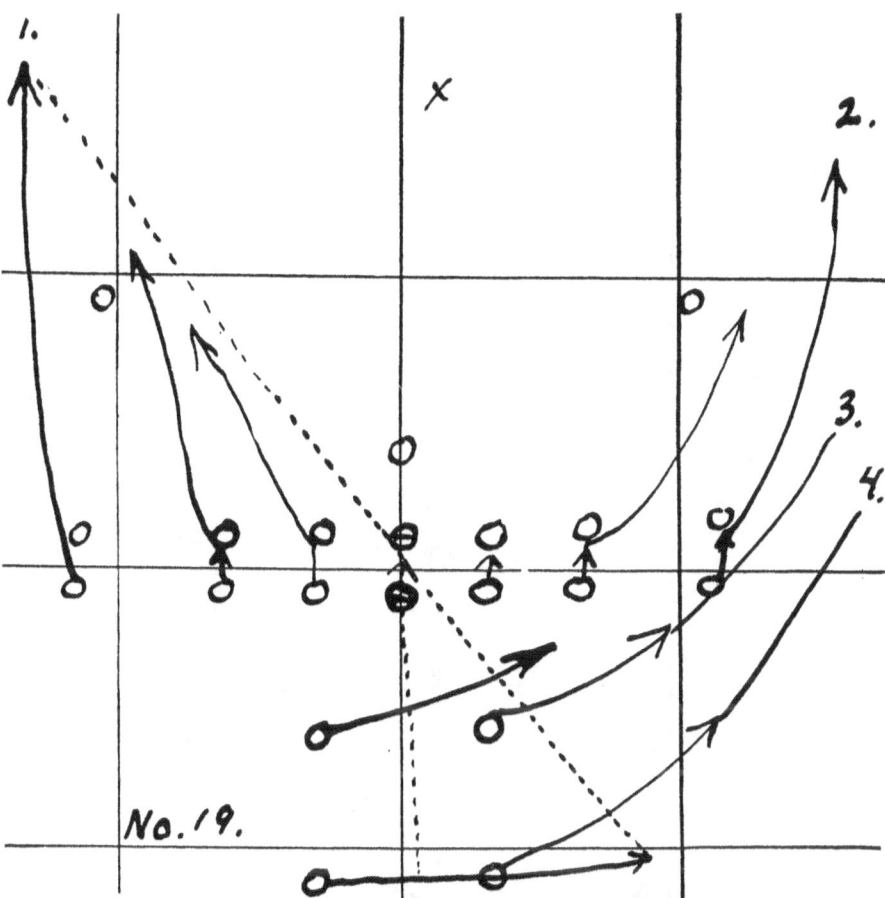

No. 19. This is a fake end run to the right and a forward pass across the line to left end marked No. 1. The play starts off like the preceeding play, but left half passes the ball after running about five to seven yards, or farther if he is not interfered with. He must, of course, pass the ball before advancing within five yards of the line. He can also pass to players marked 2, 3 or 4 if left end is covered and it might be well to have right end run to the spot marked X so that the pass could be made to that spot if the others were covered.

1910 Offense

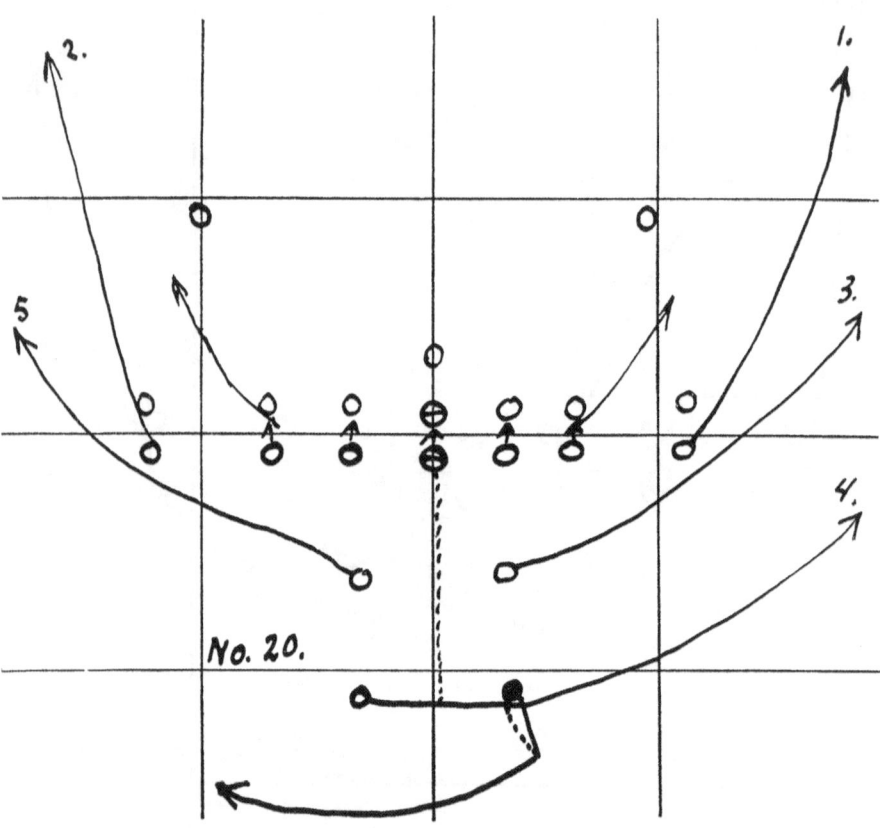

No. 20. This is a criss-cross ending in a forward pass. Left half starts to the right with the ball. Right half backs up and faces to the left and receives the ball from left half as he passes him. Right half then runs back and to the left. While these maneuvers are taking place the other backs and the ends run for uncovered positions as indicated and left half continues his run to the right. Right half can now pass the ball to No. 1, 2, 3, 4 or 5 whichever is uncovered. No. 2 seems to be the most likely place to pass to. The other line men block long and hard.

1910 Offense 69

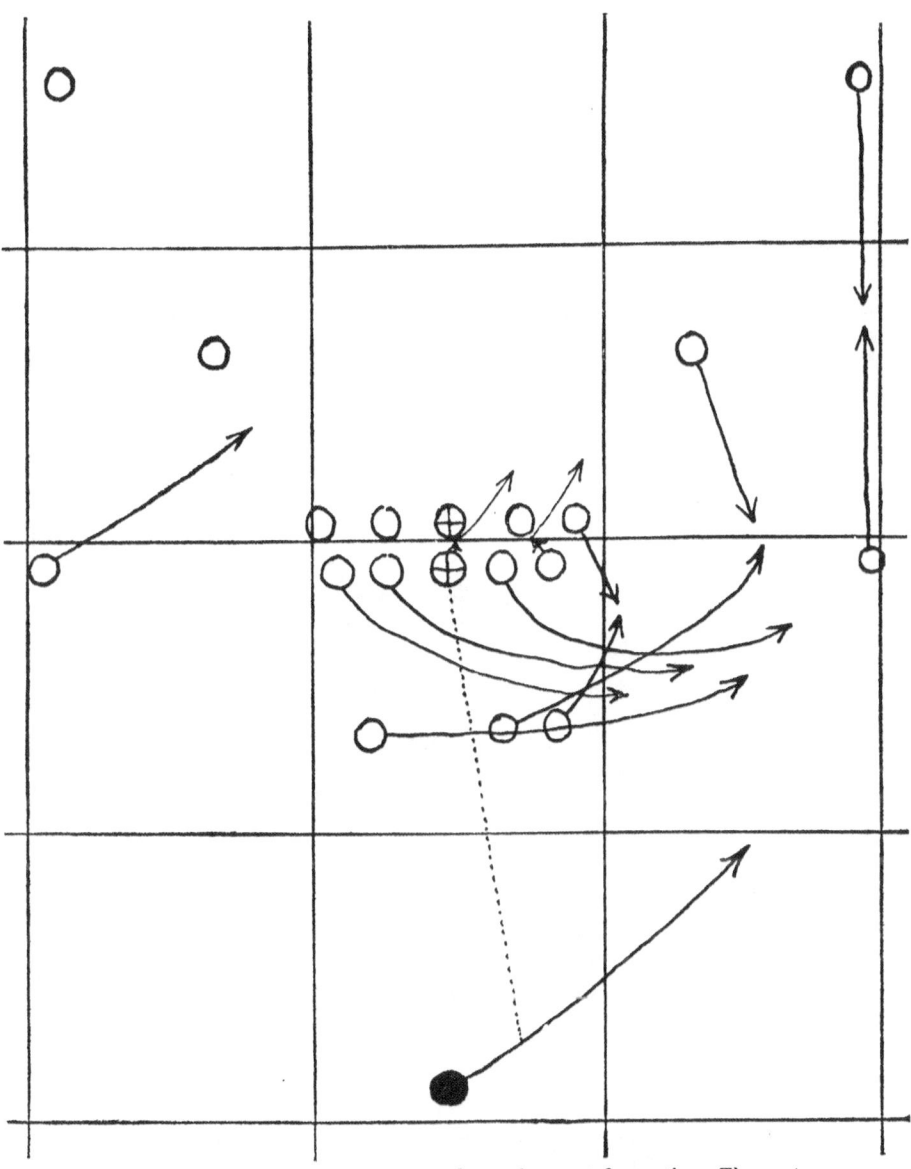

No. 21. This and the following plays are from the punt formation. The center passes the ball to the right, the punter receiving it upon the run. The line men and backs block or interfere as indicated. Speed is a great factor in this play. Note that the right guard gets into the interference, and that right half blocks the opposing tackle.

From this formation most of the punting should be done, it not being considered necessary to diagram the punt play, as the duties of the players are either apparent or are explained elsewhere in the course.

1910 Offense

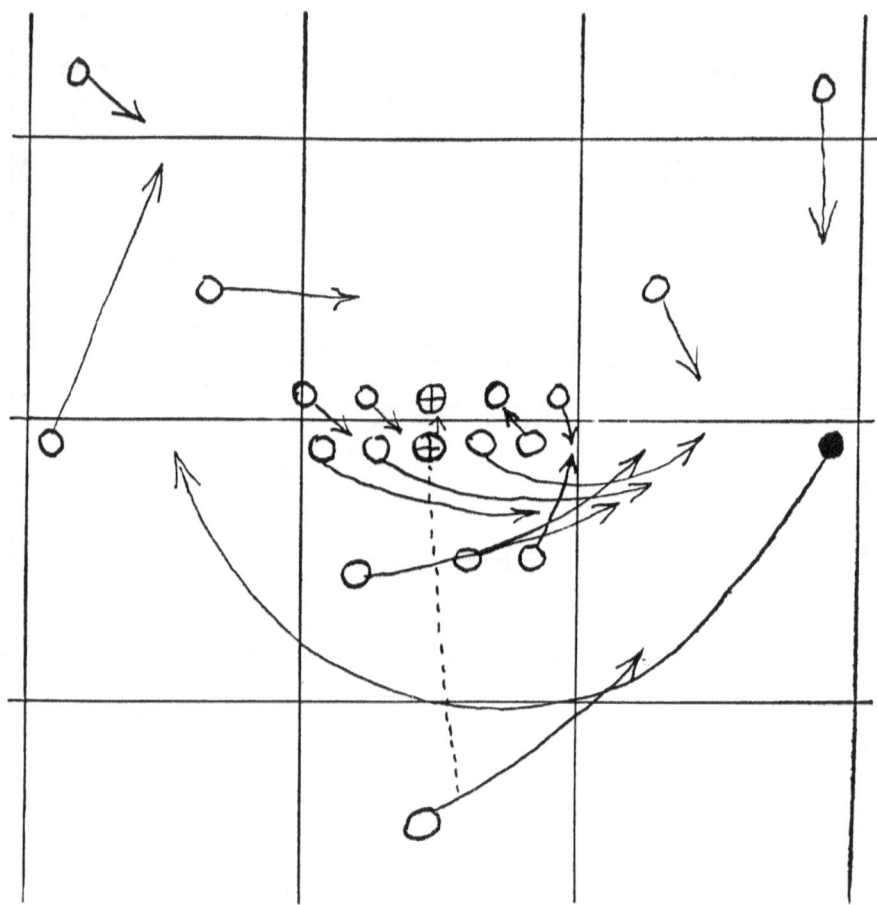

No. 22.—This play starts off like No. 21, but the man receiving the ball passes it to right end, who leaves his position with the snap of the ball and swings around the opposite end. This is a criss-cross that works.

1910 Offense

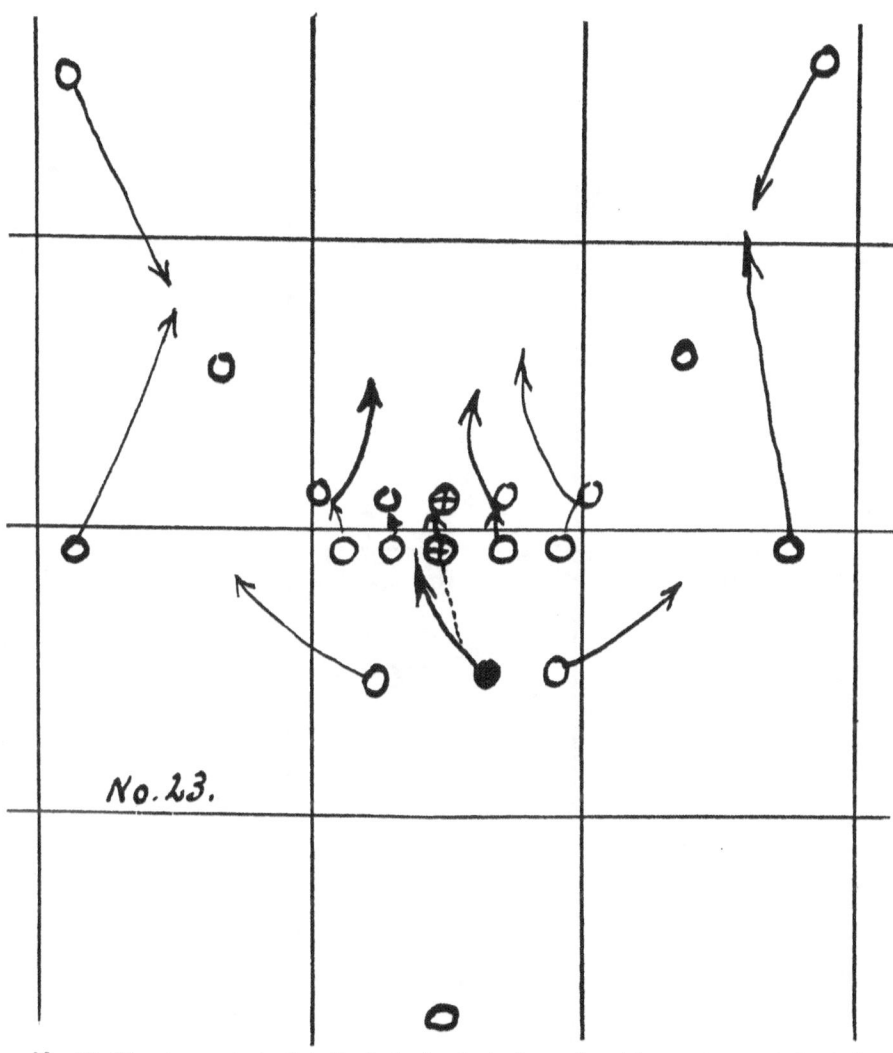

No. 23. Direct pass to back indicated who darts through quick opening made by left guard and center. The other backs run out to help draw attention away from the play. The other linemen push their opponents out and go through to block off the secondary defense.

1910 Offense

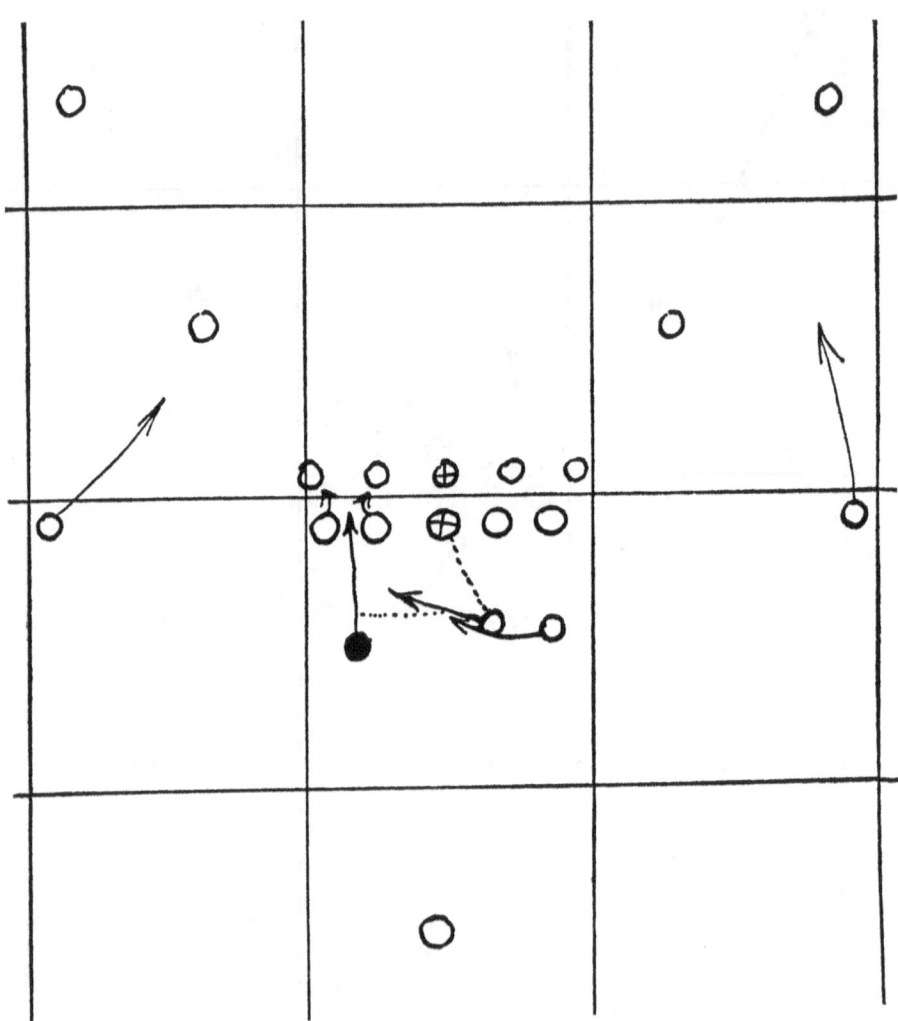

No. 24. Fake kick. The ball is passed to quarter and he passes it across to left half, who darts through the line between guard and tackle. Quarter and right half go into the line by the side of the runner to help bend the line back in case left guard and tackle are unable to make an opening.

1910 Offense

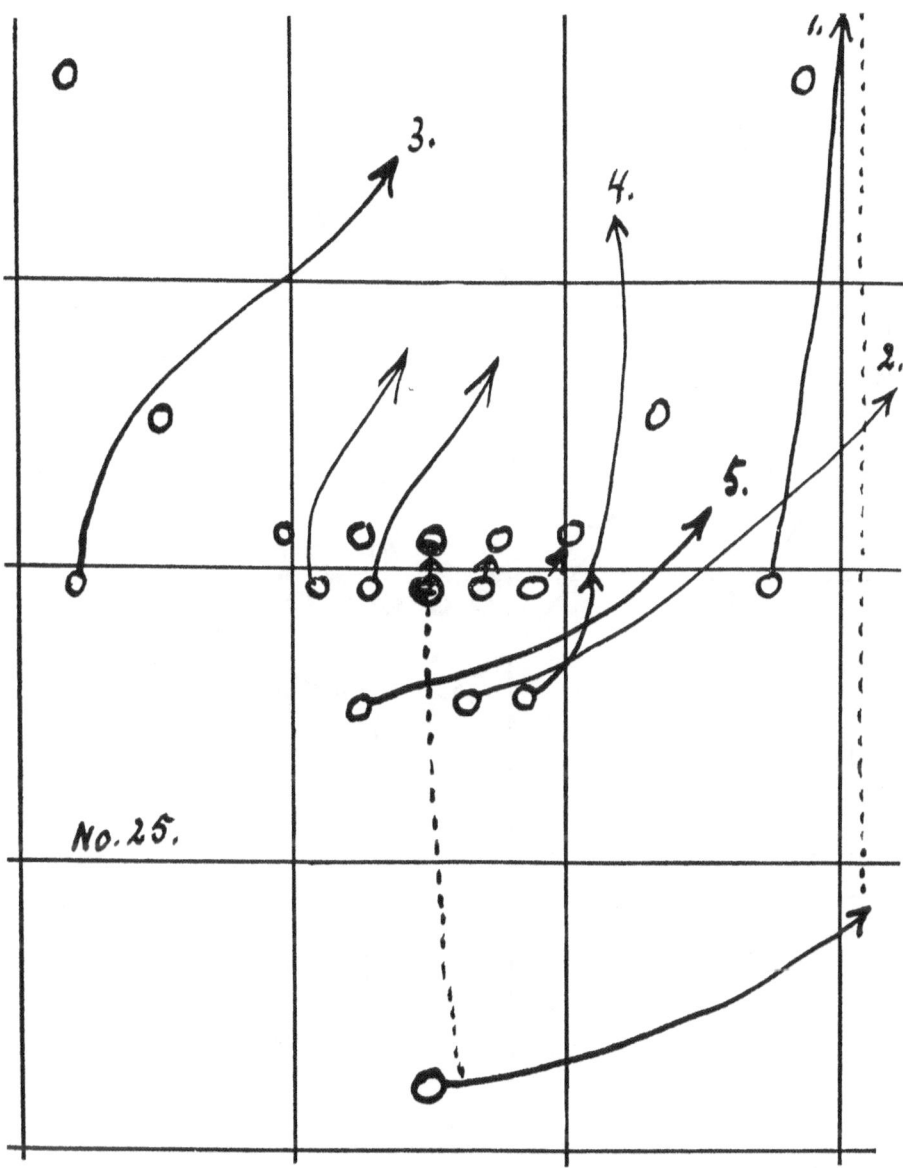

No. 25. Forward pass after a run to the right. The play is made to look like play No. 21 and the two are used to help each other and keep the opponents guessing. The player who stands back apparently for a punt secures the ball on the run from center and places it under his right arm so as to make the opponents think he intends to circle the end. When he has run well out he passes the ball either to No. 1 or to No. 2, but he can also pass to No. 3 or 4 if the others are covered. hTe pass to No. 1 will probablyprove the best play.

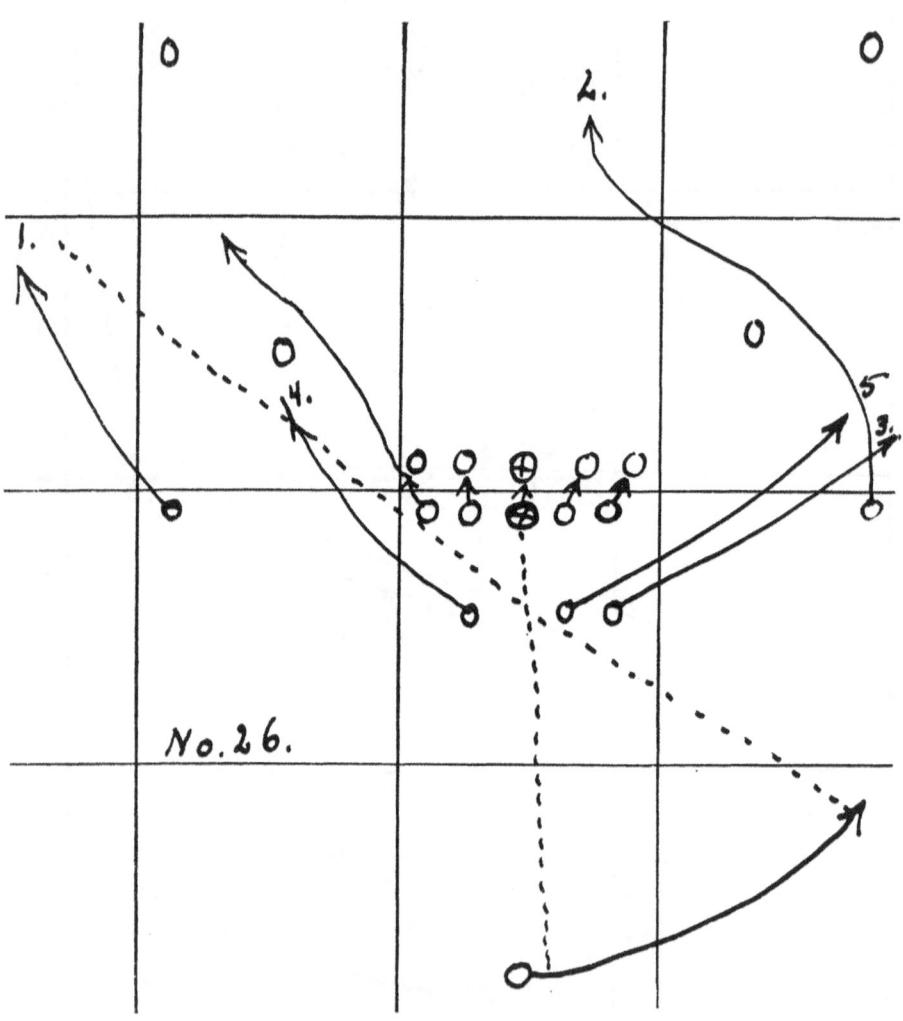

No. 26. Run to the right with a pass back across to the left end. The pass will probably work best to No. 1, but if this player is covered the pass can be made to No. 2 who should be ready to receive it. Nos. 3, 4 and 5 run as indicated so as to draw some of the defense to cover them and leave No. 1 and No. 2 uncovered.

1910 Offense

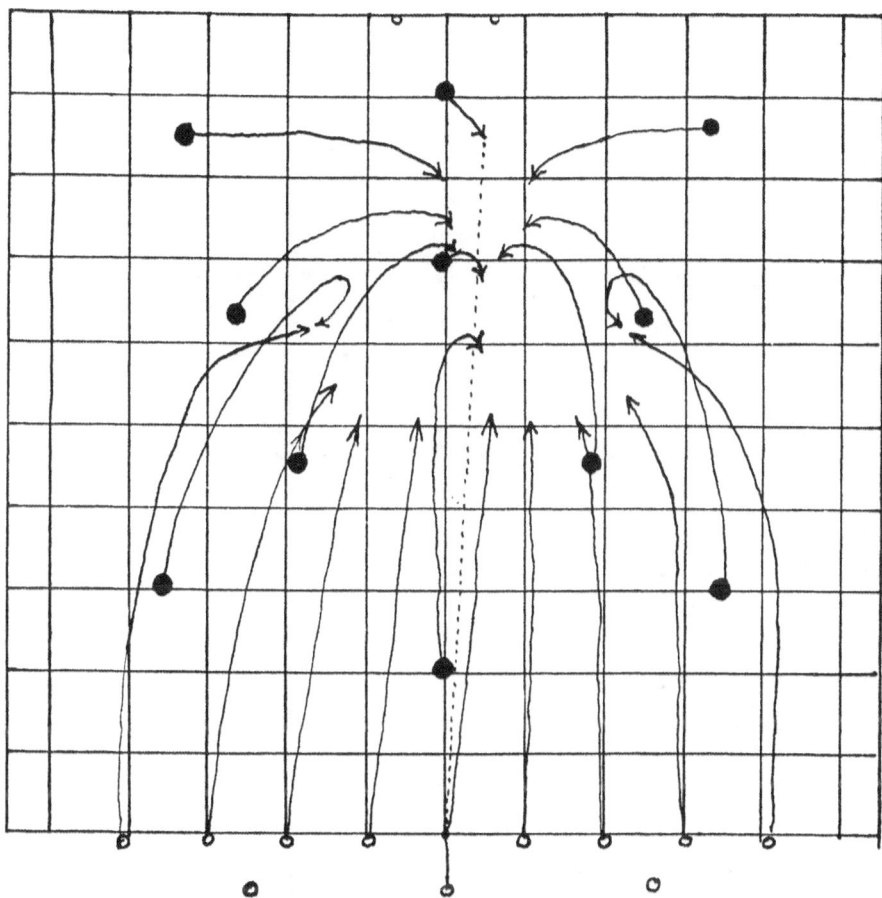

No. 27. This diagram explains a good formation and interference for running back kick-offs and kick-outs from the twenty-five yard line, and place kicks (after fair catches) which do not score or result in touchbacks.

The ends should be fifteen yards from the side line, so as to guard against short kicks to the side. Center stands ten yards from the ball, also to guard against a short kick. The diagram shows positions of all. The distance the backs should stand from the ball depends upon the wind, and upon the ability of the kicker. The whole team should run back toward the spot where the ball is to be caught, and turn in time to block opponents and form fast and close interference for the runner. The ends should keep on the inside of their opponents, and block them out as they turn in to tackle the runner. In fact all the men should endeavor to block their opponents out. Center should dodge the ball if kicked low, because if it hits him his opponents are more likely to get it than he.

On kick-outs the formation is the same, except that center stands on the twenty-five yard line and tries to block the kick.

1910 Offense

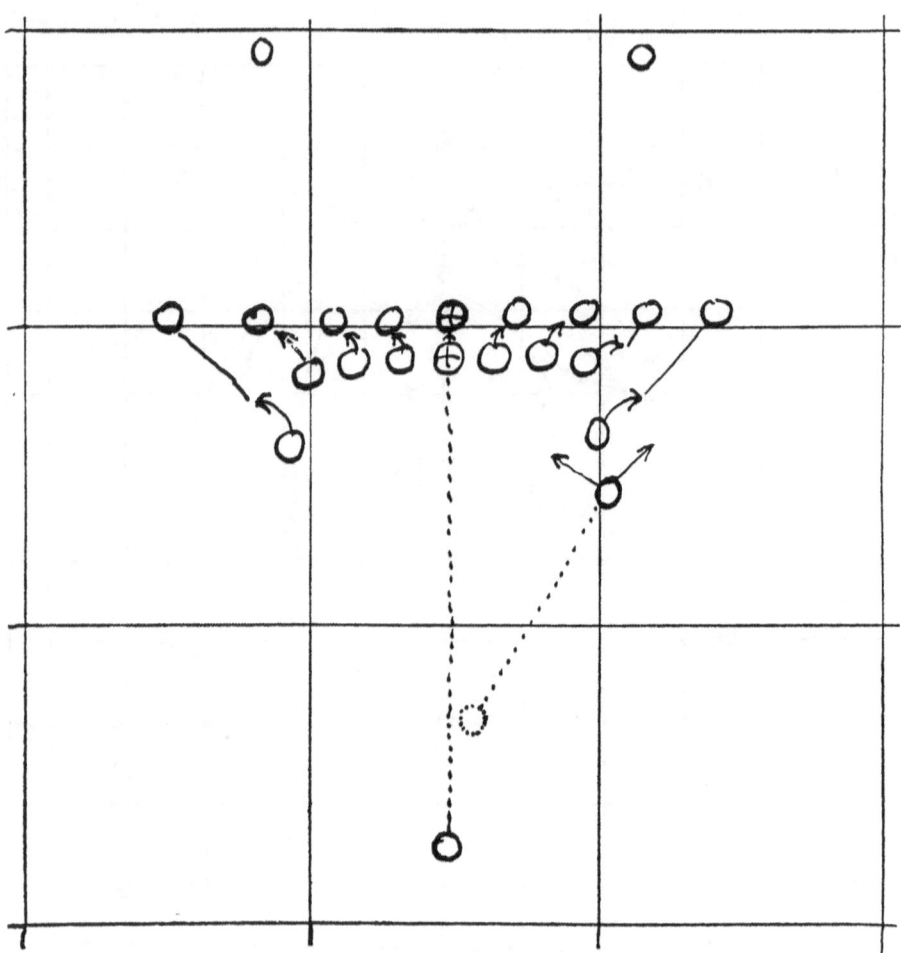

No. 28. Drop-kick or quick place-kick formation. Solid circles show formation for a drop-kick, and the dotted circle show the holder of the ball and where he should be, in case the trial is to be by a quick place-kick. Every man who is protecting the kicker (excepting the center) should make it a point to block his man outward, so that if his opponent breaks through it will be difficult for him to get in front of the ball. In case of the drop-kick, the extra back on the right should watch for and block any man coming through the center.

1910 Offense 77

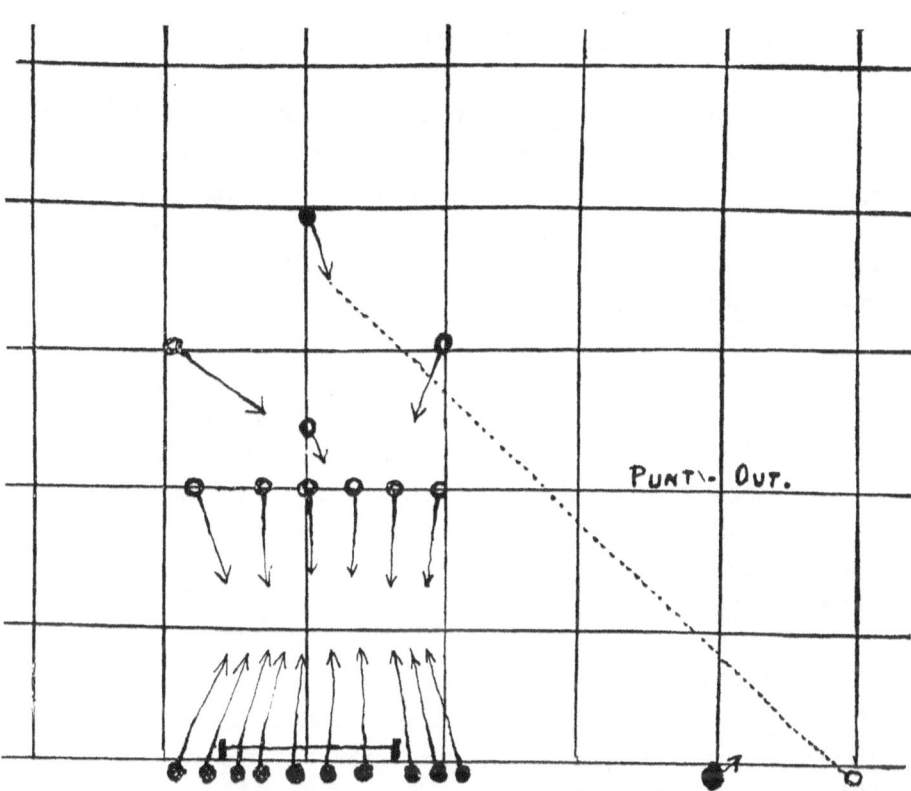

PUNT-OUT—A punt-out should be made after a touchdown in case the ball is declared dead more than ten yards to either side of the goal, and the diagram shows how the two teams should line up, although the line men of the side making the punt-out usually stand upon the five yard line instead of the ten yard line. There should be four of the best punt catchers of the punter's side stationed so as to cover the ground where the punt is likely to fall, and when one of them is sure he can catch the ball he should yell "I have it," and all the rest of his team should advance toward the opponents, so as to block them and protect the catcher.

Reprints of the Pop Warner Single-Wing Trilogy

A Course in Football for Players and Coaches: Offense
Reprints of the 1908 Offense pamphlet, 1909 supplement & 1910 revision from Warner's ground-breaking correspondence course on the rudiments of football. Also includes Tom Benjey's interpretation of the birth and early evolution of the single-wing offense.
ISBN-10 0-9774486-5-7
ISBN-13 978-0-9774486-5-4

A Course in Football for Players and Coaches
Reprint of Warner's 1912 hardbound version of his correspondence course on the rudiments of football. Includes an early evolution of the single-wing offense.
ISBN-10 0-9774486-6-5
ISBN-13 978-0-9774486-6-1

Football for Coaches and Players
Reprint of Warner's 1927 hardbound classic on the rudiments of football. Includes evolved unbalanced-line single-wing and double-wing formations.
ISBN-10 0-9774486-4-9
ISBN-13 978-0-9774486-4-7

Watch Carlisle Indian School football stars tackle bootleggers, socialites, the government, students, movie moguls and other demons while creating the professional game in Tom Benjey's upcoming book.

Tuxedo Press
546 E Springville Rd
Carlisle, PA 17015
717-258-9733
www.LoneStarDietz.com

www.ingramcontent.com/pod-product-compliance
Lightning Source LLC
Chambersburg PA
CBHW031301290426
44109CB00012B/679